FROM DARKNESS TO DOMINION: 40 Days to Break Free from the Hidden Grip of Darkness

A Global Devotional of Awareness, Deliverance & Power

For Individuals, Families, and Nations Ready to Be Free

By

Zacharias Godseagle; Ambassador Monday O. Ogbe and Comfort Ladi Ogbe

Table of Contents

About the Book – FROM DARKNESS TO DOMINION 1
Back Cover Text 3
One-Paragraph Media Promo (Press/Email/Ad Blurb) 4
Dedication 6
Acknowledgments 7
To the Reader 8
How to Use This Book 10
Preface 12
Foreword 14
Introduction 15
CHAPTER 1: ORIGINS OF THE DARK KINGDOM 18
CHAPTER 2: HOW THE DARK KINGDOM OPERATES TODAY 21
CHAPTER 3: ENTRY POINTS – HOW PEOPLE GET HOOKED 24
CHAPTER 4: MANIFESTATIONS – FROM POSSESSION TO OBSESSION 26
CHAPTER 5: THE POWER OF THE WORD – THE AUTHORITY OF BELIEVERS 28
DAY 1: BLOODLINES & GATES — BREAKING FAMILY CHAINS 31
DAY 2: DREAM INVASIONS — WHEN NIGHT BECOMES A BATTLEFIELD 34
DAY 3: SPIRITUAL SPOUSES — UNHOLY UNIONS THAT BIND DESTINIES 37
DAY 4: CURSED OBJECTS – DOORS THAT DEFILE 40
DAY 5: CHARMED & DECEIVED — BREAKING FREE FROM THE SPIRIT OF DIVINATION 43
DAY 6: GATES OF THE EYE – SHUTTING DOWN PORTALS OF DARKNESS 46
DAY 7: THE POWER BEHIND NAMES — RENOUNCING UNHOLY IDENTITIES 49

DAY 8: UNMASKING FALSE LIGHT — NEW AGE TRAPS AND ANGELIC DECEPTIONS 52
DAY 9: THE ALTAR OF BLOOD — COVENANTS THAT DEMAND A LIFE 55
DAY 10: BARRENNESS & BROKENNESS — WHEN THE WOMB BECOMES A BATTLEFIELD 58
DAY 11: AUTOIMMUNE DISORDERS & CHRONIC FATIGUE — THE INVISIBLE WAR WITHIN 61
DAY 12: EPILEPSY & MENTAL TORMENT — WHEN THE MIND BECOMES A BATTLEGROUND 64
DAY 13: SPIRIT OF FEAR — BREAKING THE CAGE OF INVISIBLE TORMENT 67
DAY 14: SATANIC MARKINGS — ERASING THE UNHOLY BRAND 70
DAY 15: THE MIRROR REALM — ESCAPING THE PRISON OF REFLECTIONS 73
DAY 16: BREAKING THE BOND OF WORD CURSES — RECLAIMING YOUR NAME, YOUR FUTURE 76
DAY 17: DELIVERANCE FROM CONTROL & MANIPULATION 79
DAY 18: BREAKING THE POWER OF UNFORGIVENESS & BITTERNESS 82
DAY 19: HEALING FROM SHAME & CONDEMNATION 85
DAY 20: HOUSEHOLD WITCHCRAFT — WHEN DARKNESS LIVES UNDER THE SAME ROOF 88
DAY 21: THE JEZEBEL SPIRIT — SEDUCTION, CONTROL, AND RELIGIOUS MANIPULATION 91
DAY 22: PYTHONS AND PRAYERS — BREAKING THE SPIRIT OF CONSTRICTION 95
DAY 23: THRONES OF INIQUITY — TEARING DOWN TERRITORIAL STRONGHOLDS 98
DAY 24: SOUL FRAGMENTS — WHEN PARTS OF YOU ARE MISSING 101
DAY 25: THE CURSE OF STRANGE CHILDREN — WHEN DESTINIES ARE EXCHANGED AT BIRTH 104

DAY 26: HIDDEN ALTARS OF POWER — BREAKING FREE FROM ELITE OCCULTIC COVENANTS 107

DAY 27: UNHOLY ALLIANCES — FREEMASONRY, ILLUMINATI & SPIRITUAL INFILTRATION 110

DAY 28: KABBALAH, ENERGY GRIDS & THE LURE OF MYSTICAL "LIGHT" 113

DAY 29: THE ILLUMINATI VEIL — UNMASKING THE ELITE OCCULT NETWORKS 116

DAY 30: THE MYSTERY SCHOOLS — ANCIENT SECRETS, MODERN BONDAGE 119

DAY 31: KABBALAH, SACRED GEOMETRY & ELITE LIGHT DECEPTION 123

DAY 32: THE SERPENT SPIRIT WITHIN — WHEN DELIVERANCE COMES TOO LATE 127

DAY 33: THE SERPENT SPIRIT WITHIN — WHEN DELIVERANCE COMES TOO LATE 131

DAY 34: MASONS, CODES & CURSES — When Brotherhood Becomes Bondage 135

DAY 35: WITCHES IN THE PEWS — WHEN EVIL ENTERS THROUGH THE CHURCH DOORS 139

DAY 36: CODED SPELLS — WHEN SONGS, FASHION & MOVIES BECOME PORTALS 143

DAY 37: THE INVISIBLE ALTARS OF POWER — FREEMASONS, KABBALAH, & OCCULT ELITES 147

DAY 38: WOMB COVENANTS & WATER KINGDOMS — WHEN DESTINY IS DEFILED BEFORE BIRTH 151

DAY 39: WATER BAPTIZED INTO BONDAGE — HOW INFANTS, INITIALS & UNSEEN COVENANTS OPEN DOORS 155

DAY 40: FROM DELIVERED TO DELIVERER — YOUR PAIN IS YOUR ORDINATION 159

360° DAILY DECLARATION OF DELIVERANCE & DOMINION – Part 1 162

360° DAILY DECLARATION OF DELIVERANCE & DOMINION – Part 2 164

360° DAILY DECLARATION OF DELIVERANCE & DOMINION - Part 3 168
CONCLUSION: FROM SURVIVAL TO SONSHIP — STAYING FREE, LIVING FREE, SETTING OTHERS FREE 172
   How to Be Born Again and Start a New Life with Christ 175
   My Salvation Moment 177
   Certificate of New Life in Christ 178
   CONNECT WITH GOD'S EAGLE MINISTRIES 180
   RECOMMENDED BOOKS & RESOURCES 182
   APPENDIX 1: Prayer to Discern Hidden Witchcraft, Occult Practices, or Strange Altars in the Church 196
   APPENDIX 2: Media Renunciation & Cleansing Protocol 197
   APPENDIX 3: Freemasonry, Kabbalah, Kundalini, Witchcraft, Occult Renunciation Script 198
   APPENDIX 4: Anointing Oil Activation Guide 199
   APPENDIX 6: Video Resources with Testimonies for spiritual growth 200
   FINAL WARNING: You Can't Play With This 201

Copyright page

FROM DARKNESS TO DOMINION: 40 Days to Break Free from the Hidden Grip of Darkness – A Global Devotional of Awareness, Deliverance & Power

By Zacharias Godseagle, Comfort Ladi Ogbe & Ambassador Monday O. Ogbe

Copyright © 2025 by **Zacharias Godseagle and God's Eagle Ministrie**s – GEM

All rights reserved.

No part of this publication may be reproduced, stored in a retrieval system, or transmitted in any form or by any means — electronic, mechanical, photocopying, recording, scanning, or otherwise — without the prior written permission of the publishers, except in the case of brief quotations embodied in critical articles or reviews.

This book is a work of nonfiction and devotional fiction. Some names and identifying details have been changed for privacy where necessary.

Scripture quotations are taken from:

- *New Living Translation (NLT)*, © 1996, 2004, 2015 by Tyndale House Foundation. Used by permission. All rights reserved.

Cover design by GEM TEAM
Interior layout by GEM TEAM
Published by:
Zacharias Godseagle & God's Eagle Ministries – GEM
www.otakada.org[1] | ambassador@otakada.org
First Edition, 2025
Printed in United States of America

---

1. http://www.otakada.org

About the Book – FROM DARKNESS TO DOMINION

FROM DARKNESS TO DOMINION: 40 Days to Break Free from the Hidden Grip of Darkness - *A Global Devotional of Awareness, Deliverance & Power - For Individuals, Families, and Nations Ready to Be Free* is not just a devotional — it's a 40-day global deliverance encounter for **Presidents, Prime Ministers, Pastors, Church Workers, CEOs, Parents, Teens, and every believer** who refuses to live in quiet defeat.

This powerful 40-day devotional addresses *spiritual warfare, deliverance from ancestral altars, breaking soul ties, occult exposure, and global testimonies from ex-witches, former satanists*, and those who've overcome the powers of darkness.

Whether you're **leading a country**, **pastoring a church**, **running a business**, or **battling for your family in the prayer closet**, this book will expose what's been hidden, confront what's been ignored, and empower you to break free.

A 40-Day Global Devotional of Awareness, Deliverance & Power
Inside these pages, you'll confront:

- Bloodline curses and ancestral covenants
- Spirit spouses, marine spirits, and astral manipulation
- Freemasonry, Kabbalah, kundalini awakenings, and witchcraft altars
- Child dedications, prenatal initiations, and demonic porters
- Media infiltration, sexual trauma, and soul fragmentation
- Secret societies, demonic AI, and false revival movements

Each day includes:
- A real story or global pattern

- Scripture-based insight
- Group and personal applications
- Deliverance prayer + reflection journal

This Book Is For You If You're:

- A **President or policymaker** seeking spiritual clarity and protection for your nation
- A **Pastor, intercessor, or church worker** battling invisible forces that resist growth and purity
- A **CEO or business leader** facing unexplainable warfare and sabotage
- A **Teen or student** plagued by dreams, torment, or strange occurrences
- A **Parent or caregiver** noticing spiritual patterns in your bloodline
- A **Christian leader** weary of endless prayer cycles with no breakthrough
- Or simply a **believer ready to go from surviving to victorious dominion**

Why This Book?

Because in a time when darkness wears the mask of light, **deliverance is no longer optional**.

And **power belongs to the informed, the equipped, and the surrendered**.

Written by Zacharias Godseagle, Ambassador Monday O. Ogbe, and Comfort Ladi Ogbe, this is more than just teaching — it's a **global wake-up call** for the Church, the family, and the nations to rise up and fight back — not in fear, but in **wisdom and authority**.

You can't disciple what you haven't delivered. And you can't walk in dominion until you break free from the grip of darkness.

Break the cycles. Confront the hidden. Take back your destiny — one day at a time.

Back Cover Text

FROM DARKNESS TO DOMINION
40 Days to Break Free from the Hidden Grip of Darkness
A Global Devotional of Awareness, Deliverance & Power

Are you a **president**, a **pastor**, a **parent**, or a **praying believer**—desperate for lasting freedom and breakthrough?

This isn't just a devotional. It's a 40-day global journey through the unseen battlefields of **ancestral covenants, occult bondage, marine spirits, soul fragmentation, media infiltration, and more**. Each day reveals real testimonies, global manifestations, and actionable deliverance strategies.

You'll uncover:

- How spiritual gates are opened—and how to shut them
- The hidden roots of repeated delay, torment, and bondage
- Powerful daily prayers, reflections, and group applications
- How-to walk-in **dominion**, not just deliverance

From **witchcraft altars** in Africa to **new age deception** in North America… from **secret societies** in Europe to **blood covenants** in Latin America—**this book exposes it all**.

DARKNESS TO DOMINION is your roadmap to liberty, written for **pastors, leaders, families, teens, professionals, CEOs**, and anyone tired of cycling through warfare without victory.

"You can't disciple what you haven't delivered. And you can't walk in dominion until you break free from the grip of darkness."

One-Paragraph Media Promo (Press/Email/Ad Blurb)

DARKNESS TO DOMINION: 40 Days to Break Free from the Hidden Grip of Darkness is a global devotional exposing how the enemy infiltrates lives, families, and nations through altars, bloodlines, secret societies, occult rituals, and everyday compromise. With stories from every continent and battle-tested deliverance strategies, this book is for presidents and pastors, CEOs and teenagers, homemakers and spiritual warriors—anyone desperate for lasting freedom. It's not just for reading—it's for breaking chains.

Suggested Tags

- deliverance devotional
- spiritual warfare
- ex-occult testimonies
- prayer and fasting
- breaking generational curses
- freedom from darkness
- Christian spiritual authority
- marine spirits
- kundalini deception
- secret societies exposed
- 40 day deliverance

 # Hashtags for Campaigns
#DarknessToDominion
#DeliveranceDevotional
#BreakTheChains
#FreedomThroughChrist

#GlobalAwakening
#HiddenBattlesExposed
#PrayToBreakFree
#SpiritualWarfareBook
#FromDarknessToLight
#KingdomAuthority
#NoMoreBondage
#ExOccultTestimonies
#KundaliniWarning
#MarineSpiritsExposed
#40DaysOfFreedom

Dedication

To the One who called us out of darkness into His marvelous light — **Jesus Christ**, our Deliverer, Light-bearer, and King of Glory.

To every soul crying out in silence — trapped by invisible chains, haunted by dreams, tormented by voices, and battling darkness in places where no one sees — this journey is for you.

To the **pastors**, **intercessors**, and **watchmen on the wall**,

To the **mothers** who pray through the night, and the **fathers** who refuse to give up,

To the **young boy** who sees too much, and the **little girl** marked by evil too early,

To the **CEOs**, **presidents**, and **decision-makers** carrying invisible weights behind public power,

To the **church worker** struggling with secret bondage, and the **spiritual warrior** who dares to fight back —

This is your call to arise.

And to the brave ones who shared their stories — thank you. Your scars now set others free.

May this devotional light a path through the shadows and lead many into dominion, healing, and holy fire.

You are not forgotten. You are not powerless.

You were born for freedom.

— *Zacharias Godseagle, Ambassador Monday O. Ogbe & Comfort Ladi Ogbe*

Acknowledgments

First and foremost, we acknowledge **God Almighty — Father, Son, and Holy Spirit**, the Author of Light and Truth, who opened our eyes to the unseen battles behind closed doors, veils, pulpits, and platforms. To Jesus Christ, our Deliverer and King, we give all glory.

To the brave men and women around the world who shared their stories of torment, triumph, and transformation — your courage has ignited a global wave of freedom. Thank you for breaking the silence.

To the ministries and watchmen on the wall who have labored in hidden places — teaching, interceding, delivering, and discerning — we honor your persistence. Your obedience continues to tear down strongholds and unmask deception in high places.

To our families, prayer partners, and support teams who stood with us while we dug through spiritual rubble to uncover truth — thank you for your unwavering faith and patience.

To researchers, YouTube testimonies, whistleblowers, and kingdom warriors who expose darkness through their platforms — your boldness has fed this work with insight, revelation, and urgency.

To the **Body of Christ**: this book is also yours. May it awaken in you a holy resolve to be vigilant, discerning, and fearless. We write not as experts, but as witnesses. We stand not as judges, but as those redeemed.

And finally, to the **readers of this devotional** — seekers, warriors, pastors, deliverance ministers, survivors, and truth lovers from every nation — may every page empower you to move **From darkness to dominion**.

— **Zacharias Godseagle**

— **Ambassador Monday O. Ogbe**

— **Comfort Ladi Ogbe**

To the Reader

This is not just a book. It is a call.

A call to uncover what has long been hidden — to confront the invisible forces shaping generations, systems, and souls. Whether you are a **young seeker**, a **pastor worn from battles you can't name**, a **business leader battling night terrors**, or a **head of state facing unrelenting national darkness**, this devotional is your **guide out of the shadows**.

To the **individual**: You are not crazy. What you sense — in your dreams, your atmosphere, your bloodline — may indeed be spiritual. God is not just a healer; He is a deliverer.

To the **family**: This 40-day journey will help you identify patterns that have long tormented your bloodline — addictions, untimely deaths, divorces, barrenness, mental torment, sudden poverty — and provide the tools to break them.

To **church leaders and pastors**: May this awaken a deeper discernment and courage to confront the spirit realm from the pulpit, not just the podium. Deliverance is not optional. It is part of the Great Commission.

To **CEOs, entrepreneurs, and professionals**: Spiritual covenants operate in boardrooms too. Dedicate your business to God. Tear down ancestral altars disguised as business luck, blood pacts, or Freemason favor. Build with clean hands.

To the **watchmen and intercessors**: Your vigilance has not been in vain. This resource is a weapon in your hands — for your city, your region, your nation.

To **Presidents and Prime Ministers**, if this ever reaches your desk: Nations are not just governed by policies. They are ruled by altars — raised in secret or public. Until the hidden foundations are addressed, peace will remain elusive. May this devotional stir you toward a generational reformation.

To the **young man or woman** reading this in a moment of desperation: God sees you. He chose you. And He's pulling you out — for good.

This is your journey. One day at a time. One chain at a time.

From Darkness to Dominion — it's your time.

How to Use This Book

FROM DARKNESS TO DOMINION: 40 Days to Break Free from the Hidden Grip of Darkness is more than a devotional — it is a deliverance manual, a spiritual detox, and a warfare boot camp. Whether you're reading alone, with a group, in a church, or as a leader guiding others, here's how to get the most out of this powerful 40-day journey:

Daily Rhythm

Each day follows a consistent structure to help you engage spirit, soul, and body:

- **Main Devotional Teaching** – A revelatory theme exposing hidden darkness.
- **Global Context** – How this stronghold manifests around the world.
- **Real-Life Stories** – True deliverance encounters from different cultures.
- **Action Plan** – Personal spiritual exercises, renunciation, or declarations.
- **Group Application** – For use in small groups, families, churches, or deliverance teams.
- **Key Insight** – A distilled takeaway to remember and pray into.
- **Reflection Journal** – Heart questions to process each truth deeply.
- **Prayer of Deliverance** – Targeted spiritual warfare prayer to break strongholds.

What You'll Need

- Your **Bible**
- A **dedicated journal or notebook**

- **Anointing oil** (optional but powerful during prayers)
- Willingness to **fast and pray** as the Spirit leads
- **Accountability partner or prayer team** for deeper cases

How to Use with Groups or Churches

- Meet **daily or weekly** to discuss insights and lead prayers together.
- Encourage members to complete the **Reflection Journal** before group sessions.
- Use the **Group Application** section to spark discussion, confession, or corporate deliverance moments.
- Designate trained leaders to handle more intense manifestations.

For Pastors, Leaders, and Deliverance Ministers

- Teach the daily topics from the pulpit or in deliverance training schools.
- Equip your team to use this devotional as a counseling guide.
- Customize sections as needed for spiritual mapping, revival meetings, or city prayer drives.

Appendices to Explore
At the end of the book, you'll find powerful bonus resources, including:

1. **Daily Declaration of Total Deliverance** – Speak this aloud every morning and night.
2. **Media Renunciation Guide** – Detox your life from spiritual contamination in entertainment.
3. **Prayer to Discern Hidden Altars in Churches** – For intercessors and church workers.
4. **Freemasonry, Kabbalah, Kundalini & Occult Renunciation Script** – Powerful repentance prayers.
5. **Mass Deliverance Checklist** – Use in crusades, house fellowships, or personal retreats.
6. **Testimony Video Links**

Preface

There is a war — unseen, unspoken, but fiercely real — raging over the souls of men, women, children, families, communities, and nations.

This book was born not from theory, but from fire. From weeping deliverance rooms. From testimonies whispered in shadows and shouted from rooftops. From deep study, global intercession, and a holy frustration with surface-level Christianity that fails to deal with the **roots of darkness** still entangling believers.

Too many people have come to the cross but are still dragging chains. Too many pastors are preaching liberty while secretly tormented by demons of lust, fear, or ancestral covenants. Too many families are trapped in cycles — of poverty, perversion, addiction, barrenness, shame — and **don't know why**. And far too many churches avoid talking about demons, witchcraft, blood altars, or deliverance because it's "too intense."

But Jesus didn't avoid darkness — He **confronted it**.

He didn't ignore demons — He **cast them out**.

And He didn't die just to forgive you — He died to **free you**.

This 40-day global devotional is not a casual Bible study. It is a **spiritual operation room**. A journal of freedom. A map out of hell for those who feel stuck between salvation and true liberty. Whether you are a teenager bound by pornography, a First Lady plagued by dreams of serpents, a Prime Minister tormented by ancestral guilt, a prophet hiding secret bondage, or a child waking up from demonic dreams — this journey is for you.

You will find stories from around the world — Africa, Asia, Europe, North and South America — all confirming one truth: **the devil is no respecter of persons**. But neither is God. And what He has done for others, He can do for you.

This book is written for:

- **Individuals** seeking personal deliverance
- **Families** needing generational healing
- **Pastors** and church workers needing equipping
- **Business leaders** navigating spiritual warfare in high places
- **Nations** crying out for true revival
- **Youth** who have unknowingly opened doors
- **Deliverance ministers** who need structure and strategy
- And even **those who don't believe in demons** — until they read their own story on these pages

You will be stretched. You will be challenged. But if you stay on the path, you will also be **transformed**.

You're not just going to break free.

You're going to **walk in dominion**.

Let's begin.

— *Zacharias Godseagle, Ambassador Monday O. Ogbe, and Comfort Ladi Ogbe*

Foreword

There is a stirring in the nations. A shaking in the spirit realm. From pulpits to parliaments, living rooms to underground churches, people everywhere are awakening to a chilling truth: we've underestimated the reach of the enemy — and we've misunderstood the authority we carry in Christ.

From Darkness to Dominion is not just a devotional; it is a clarion call. A prophetic manual. A lifeline for the tormented, the bound, and the sincere believer wondering, "Why am I still in chains?"

As someone who has witnessed revival and deliverance across nations, I know firsthand that the Church is not lacking in knowledge — we are lacking in spiritual **awareness**, **boldness**, and **discipline**. This work bridges that gap. It weaves together global testimonies, hard-hitting truth, practical action, and the power of the cross into a 40-day journey that will shake the dust-off dormant lives and ignite fire in the weary.

To the pastor who dares to confront altars, to the young adult silently battling demonic dreams, to the business owner entangled in unseen covenants, and to the leader who knows something is *spiritually wrong* but can't name it — this book is for you.

I urge you not to read it passively. Let every page provoke your spirit. Let every story birth warfare. Let every declaration train your mouth to speak with fire. And when you've walked through these 40 days, don't just celebrate your freedom — become a vessel for the freedom of others.

Because true dominion is not just escaping darkness...

It is turning around and dragging others into the light.

In Christ's Authority and Power,
Ambassador Ogbe

Introduction

FROM DARKNESS TO DOMINION: 40 Days to Break Free from the Hidden Grip of Darkness is not just another devotional—it's a global wake-up call.

All over the world—from rural villages to presidential palaces, church altars to boardrooms—men and women are crying out for freedom. Not just salvation. **Deliverance. Clarity. Breakthrough. Wholeness. Peace. Power.**

But here's the truth: You cannot cast out what you tolerate. You cannot break free from what you cannot see. This book is your light in that darkness.

For 40 days, you will walk through teachings, stories, testimonies, and strategic actions that expose the hidden operations of darkness and empower you to overcome—spirit, soul, and body.

Whether you are a pastor, CEO, missionary, intercessor, teenager, mother, or head of state, the content of this book will confront you. Not to shame you—but to liberate you and prepare you to walk others into freedom.

This is a **global devotional of awareness, deliverance, and power**—rooted in scripture, sharpened by real-life accounts, and drenched in the blood of Jesus.

How to Use This Devotional

1. **Start with the 5 Foundational Chapters**
   These chapters lay the groundwork. Don't skip them. They will help you understand the spiritual architecture of darkness and the authority you've been given to rise above it.
2. **Walk Through Each Day Intentionally**
   Each daily entry includes a focus theme, global manifestations, a real story, scriptures, an action plan, group application ideas, key insight, journal prompts, and a powerful prayer.
3. **Close Every Day With the Daily 360° Declaration**

Found at the end of this book, this powerful declaration is designed to reinforce your freedom and shield your spiritual gates.

4. **Use It Alone or in Groups**
   Whether you're going through this individually or in a group, home fellowship, intercessory team, or deliverance ministry—allow the Holy Spirit to guide the pace and personalize the battle plan.

5. **Expect Opposition—and Breakthrough**
   Resistance will come. But so will freedom. Deliverance is a process, and Jesus is committed to walking it with you.

FOUNDATIONAL CHAPTERS (Read Before Day 1)

1. Origins of the Dark Kingdom

From Lucifer's rebellion to the emergence of demonic hierarchies and territorial spirits, this chapter traces the biblical and spiritual history of darkness. Understanding where it started helps you recognize how it operates.

2. How the Dark Kingdom Operates Today

From covenants and blood sacrifices to altars, marine spirits, and technological infiltration, this chapter uncovers the modern faces of ancient spirits—including how media, trends, and even religion can serve as camouflage.

3. Entry Points: How People Get Hooked

No one is born into bondage by accident. This chapter examines doorways such as trauma, ancestral altars, witchcraft exposure, soul ties, occult curiosity, Freemasonry, false spirituality, and cultural practices.

4. Manifestations: From Possession to Obsession

What does bondage look like? From nightmares to marital delay, infertility, addiction, rage, and even "holy laughter," this chapter reveals how demons disguise themselves as problems, gifts, or personalities.

5. The Power of the Word: Authority of Believers

Before we begin the 40-day warfare, you must understand your legal rights in Christ. This chapter arms you with spiritual laws, weapons of warfare, scriptural protocols, and the language of deliverance.

A FINAL ENCOURAGEMENT BEFORE YOU BEGIN

God is not calling you to *manage* darkness.

He is calling you to **dominate** it.

Not by might, not by power, but by His Spirit.
Let these next 40 days be more than a devotional.
Let it be a funeral for every altar that once controlled you...
and a coronation into the destiny God ordained for you.
Your dominion journey begins now.

CHAPTER 1: ORIGINS OF THE DARK KINGDOM

"*For we wrestle not against flesh and blood, but against principalities, against powers, against the rulers of the darkness of this world, against spiritual wickedness in high places.*" — Ephesians 6:12

Long before humanity stepped onto the stage of time, an invisible war broke out in the heavens. This was not a war of swords or guns, but of rebellion — a high treason against the holiness and authority of the Most High God. The Bible unveils this mystery through various passages that hint at the fall of one of God's most beautiful angels — **Lucifer**, the shining one — who dared to exalt himself above the throne of God (Isaiah 14:12–15, Ezekiel 28:12–17).

This cosmic rebellion birthed the **Dark Kingdom** — a realm of spiritual resistance and deception, made up of fallen angels (now demons), principalities, and powers aligned against God's will and God's people.

The Fall and Formation of Darkness

LUCIFER WAS NOT ALWAYS evil. He was created perfect in wisdom and beauty. But pride entered his heart, and pride became rebellion. He deceived a third of heaven's angels to follow him (Revelation 12:4), and they were cast out of heaven. Their hatred toward humanity is rooted in jealousy — because mankind was created in God's image and given dominion.

Thus began the war between the **Kingdom of Light** and the **Kingdom of Darkness** — an unseen conflict that touches every soul, every home, and every nation.

The Dark Kingdom's Global Expression

THOUGH INVISIBLE, THE influence of this dark kingdom is deeply embedded in:

- **Cultural traditions** (ancestral worship, blood sacrifices, secret societies)
- **Entertainment** (subliminal messaging, occult music & shows)
- **Governance** (corruption, blood pacts, oaths)
- **Technology** (tools for addiction, control, mind manipulation)
- **Education** (humanism, relativism, false enlightenment)

From African juju to Western new age mysticism, from Middle Eastern jinn worship to South American shamanism, the forms differ but the **spirit is the same** — deception, domination, and destruction.

Why This Book Matters Now

SATAN'S GREATEST TRICK is to make people believe he doesn't exist — or worse, that his ways are harmless.

This devotional is a **spiritual intelligence manual** — lifting the veil, exposing his schemes, and empowering believers across continents to:

- **Recognize** entry points
- **Renounce** hidden covenants
- **Resist** with authority
- **Recover** what was stolen

You Were Born into a Battle

THIS IS NOT A DEVOTIONAL for the faint-hearted. You were born into a battlefield, not a playground. But the good news is: **Jesus has already won the war!**

"He disarmed the rulers and authorities and put them to open shame, by triumphing over them in Him." — Colossians 2:15

You are not a victim. You are more than a conqueror through Christ. Let's expose the darkness — and walk boldly into the light.

Key Insight

The origin of darkness is pride, rebellion, and the rejection of God's rule. These same seeds still operate in the hearts of people and systems today. To understand spiritual warfare, we must first understand how the rebellion began.

Reflection Journal

- Have I dismissed spiritual warfare as superstition?
- What cultural or family practices have I normalized that may be tied to ancient rebellion?
- Do I truly understand the war I was born into?

Prayer of Illumination
Heavenly Father, reveal to me the hidden roots of rebellion around and within me. Expose the lies of darkness I may have embraced unknowingly. Let Your truth shine into every shadowy place. I choose the Kingdom of Light. I choose to walk in truth, power, and freedom. In Jesus' name. Amen.

CHAPTER 2: HOW THE DARK KINGDOM OPERATES TODAY

"*Lest Satan should get an advantage of us: for we are not ignorant of his devices.*" — 2 Corinthians 2:11

The kingdom of darkness does not operate haphazardly. It is a well-organized, deeply layered spiritual infrastructure that mirrors military strategy. Its goal: infiltrate, manipulate, control, and ultimately destroy. Just as the Kingdom of God has rank and order (apostles, prophets, etc.), so does the kingdom of darkness — with principalities, powers, rulers of darkness, and spiritual wickedness in high places (Ephesians 6:12).

The Dark Kingdom is not a myth. It is not folklore or religious superstition. It is an invisible but real network of spiritual agents that manipulate systems, people, and even churches to fulfill Satan's agenda. While many imagine pitchforks and red horns, the real operation of this kingdom is far more subtle, systematic, and sinister.

1. Deception is Their Currency

The enemy trades in lies. From the Garden of Eden (Genesis 3) to present-day philosophies, Satan's tactics have always revolved around planting doubt in God's Word. Today, deception appears in the form of:

- *New Age teachings disguised as enlightenment*
- *Occult practices masked as cultural pride*
- *Witchcraft glamorized in music, movies, cartoons, and social media trends*

People unknowingly participate in rituals or consume media that open spiritual doors without discernment.

2. Hierarchical Structure of Evil

Just as God's Kingdom has order, the dark kingdom operates under a defined hierarchy:

- **Principalities** – Territorial spirits influencing nations and governments
- **Powers** – Agents who enforce wickedness through demonic systems
- **Rulers of Darkness** – Coordinators of spiritual blindness, idolatry, false religion
- **Spiritual Wickedness in High Places** – Elite-level entities influencing global culture, wealth, and technology

Each demon specializes in certain assignments — fear, addiction, sexual perversion, confusion, pride, division.

3. Tools of Cultural Control

The devil no longer needs to appear physically. The culture now does the heavy lifting. His strategies today include:

- **Subliminal Messaging:** Music, shows, advertisements full of hidden symbols and reversed messages
- **Desensitization:** Repeated exposure to sin (violence, nudity, profanity) until it becomes "normal"
- **Mind Control Techniques:** Through media hypnosis, emotional manipulation, and addictive algorithms

This is not accidental. These are strategies designed to weaken moral convictions, destroy families, and redefine truth.

4. Generational Agreements & Bloodlines

Through dreams, rituals, dedications, or ancestral pacts, many people are unknowingly aligned with darkness. Satan capitalizes on:

- Family altars and ancestral idols
- Naming ceremonies invoking spirits
- Secret family sins or curses passed down

These open legal grounds for affliction until the covenant is broken by the blood of Jesus.

5. False Miracles, False Prophets

The Dark Kingdom loves religion — especially if it lacks truth and power. False prophets, seducing spirits, and counterfeit miracles deceive the masses:

"For Satan himself transforms into an angel of light." — 2 Corinthians 11:14

Many today follow voices that tickle their ears but bind their souls.

Key Insight

The devil isn't always loud — sometimes he whispers through compromise. The Dark Kingdom's greatest tactic is to convince people they are free, while they are subtly enslaved.

Reflection Journal:

- Where have you seen these operations in your community or nation?
- Are there shows, music, apps, or rituals you've normalized that may actually be tools of manipulation?

Prayer of Awareness & Repentance:

Lord Jesus, open my eyes to see the operations of the enemy. Expose every lie I've believed. Forgive me for every door I've opened, knowingly or unknowingly. I break agreement with darkness and choose Your truth, Your power, and Your freedom. In Jesus' name. Amen.

CHAPTER 3: ENTRY POINTS – HOW PEOPLE GET HOOKED

"*Do not give the devil a foothold.*" — Ephesians 4:27

In every culture, generation, and home, there are hidden openings — gateways through which spiritual darkness enters. These entry points may seem harmless at first: a childhood game, a family ritual, a book, a movie, an unresolved trauma. But once opened, they become legal ground for demonic influence.

Common Entry Points

1. **Bloodline Covenants** – Ancestral oaths, rituals, and idolatry that pass down access to evil spirits.
2. **Early Exposure to Occult** – As in the story of *Lourdes Valdivia* from Bolivia, children exposed to witchcraft, spiritualism, or occult rituals often become spiritually compromised.
3. **Media & Music** – Songs and films that glorify darkness, sensuality, or rebellion can subtly invite spiritual influence.
4. **Trauma and Abuse** – Sexual abuse, violent trauma, or rejection can crack the soul open to oppressive spirits.
5. **Sexual Sin & Soul Ties** – Illicit sexual unions often create spiritual bonds and transference of spirits.
6. **New Age & False Religion** – Crystals, yoga, spirit guides, horoscopes, and "white witchcraft" are veiled invitations.
7. **Bitterness & Unforgiveness** – These give demonic spirits a legal right to torment (see Matthew 18:34).

Global Testimony Highlight: *Lourdes Valdivia (Bolivia)*

At just 7 years old, Lourdes was introduced to witchcraft by her mother, a long-time occultist. Her house was filled with symbols, bones from cemeteries, and magic books. She experienced astral projection, voices, and torment before finally finding Jesus and being set free. Her story is one of many — proving how early exposure and generational influence open doors to spiritual bondage.

Greater Exploits Reference:

Stories of how people unknowingly opened doors through "harmless" activities — only to be ensnared in darkness — can be found in *Greater Exploits 14* and *Delivered from the Power of Darkness*.(Check appendix)

Key Insight

The enemy rarely barges in. He waits for a door to be cracked open. What feels innocent, inherited, or entertaining can sometimes be the very gate the enemy needs.

Reflection Journal

- What moments in my life may have served as spiritual entry points?
- Are there "harmless" traditions or objects I need to let go of?
- Do I need to renounce anything from my past or family line?

Prayer of Renunciation

Father, I close every door I or my ancestors may have opened to darkness. I renounce all agreements, soul ties, and exposures to anything unholy. I break every chain by the blood of Jesus. I declare my body, soul, and spirit belong to Christ alone. In Jesus' name. Amen.

CHAPTER 4: MANIFESTATIONS – FROM POSSESSION TO OBSESSION

"*When an impure spirit comes out of a person, it goes through arid places seeking rest and does not find it. Then it says, 'I will return to the house I left.'*" — Matthew 12:43

Once a person comes under the influence of the dark kingdom, manifestations vary based on the level of demonic access granted. The spiritual enemy doesn't settle for visitation — his ultimate aim is habitation and domination.

Levels of Manifestation

1. **Influence** – The enemy gains influence through thoughts, emotions, and decisions.
2. **Oppression** – There's external pressure, heaviness, confusion, and torment.
3. **Obsession** – The person becomes fixated on dark thoughts or compulsive behavior.
4. **Possession** – In rare but real cases, demons take residence and override a person's will, voice, or body.

The degree of manifestation is often connected to the depth of spiritual compromise.

Global Case Studies of Manifestation

- **Africa:** Cases of spirit husband/wife, madness, ritual servitude.
- **Europe:** New age hypnosis, astral projection, and mind fragmentation.
- **Asia:** Ancestral soul ties, reincarnation traps, and bloodline vows.

- **South America:** Shamanism, spirit guides, psychic reading addiction.
- **North America:** Witchcraft in media, "harmless" horoscopes, substance gateways.
- **Middle East:** Djinn encounters, blood oaths, and prophetic counterfeits.

Each continent presents its unique disguise of the same demonic system — and believers must learn how to recognize the signs.

Common Symptoms of Demonic Activity

- Recurring nightmares or sleep paralysis
- Voices or mental torment
- Compulsive sin and repeated backsliding
- Unexplained illnesses, fear, or rage
- Supernatural strength or knowledge
- Sudden aversion to spiritual things

Key Insight

What we call "mental," "emotional," or "medical" issues may sometimes be spiritual. Not always — but often enough that discernment is crucial.

Reflection Journal

- Have I noticed repetitive struggles that seem spiritual in nature?
- Are there generational patterns of destruction in my family?
- What kind of media, music, or relationships am I allowing into my life?

Prayer of Renunciation

Lord Jesus, I renounce every hidden agreement, open door, and ungodly covenant in my life. I break ties with anything not of You — knowingly or unknowingly. I invite the fire of the Holy Spirit to consume every trace of darkness in my life. Set me free completely. In Your mighty name. Amen.

CHAPTER 5: THE POWER OF THE WORD – THE AUTHORITY OF BELIEVERS

"*Behold, I give unto you power to tread on serpents and scorpions, and over all the power of the enemy: and nothing shall by any means hurt you.*" — Luke 10:19 (KJV)

Many believers live in fear of darkness because they do not understand the light they carry. Yet Scripture reveals that the **Word of God is not only a sword (Ephesians 6:17)** — it is fire (Jeremiah 23:29), a hammer, a seed, and life itself. In the battle between light and darkness, those who know and declare the Word are never victims.

What Is This Power?

The power believers carry is **delegated authority**. Like a police officer with a badge, we stand not on our own strength, but in the **name of Jesus** and through the Word of God. When Jesus defeated Satan in the wilderness, He didn't shout, cry, or panic — He simply said: *"It is written."*

This is the pattern for all spiritual warfare.

Why Many Christians Remain Defeated

1. **Ignorance** – They don't know what the Word says about their identity.
2. **Silence** – They don't declare God's Word over situations.
3. **Inconsistency** – They live in cycles of sin, which erodes confidence and access.

Victory is not about shouting louder; it's about **believing deeper** and **declaring boldly**.

Authority in Action – Global Stories

- **Nigeria:** A young boy trapped in cultism was delivered when his mother consistently anointed his room and spoke Psalm 91 nightly.
- **United States:** A former Wiccan abandoned witchcraft after a colleague quietly declared scriptures over her workspace daily for months.
- **India:** A believer declared Isaiah 54:17 while facing constant black magic attacks — the assaults stopped, and the attacker confessed.
- **Brazil:** A woman used daily declarations of Romans 8 over her suicidal thoughts and began walking in supernatural peace.

The Word is alive. It does not need our perfection, just our faith and confession.

How to Wield the Word in Warfare

1. **Memorize Scriptures** related to identity, victory, and protection.
2. **Speak the Word aloud**, especially during spiritual attacks.
3. **Use it in prayer**, declaring God's promises over situations.
4. **Fast + Pray** with the Word as your anchor (Matthew 17:21).

Foundational Scriptures for Warfare

- *2 Corinthians 10:3–5* – Pulling down strongholds
- *Isaiah 54:17* – No weapon formed shall prosper
- *Luke 10:19* – Power over the enemy
- *Psalm 91* – Divine protection
- *Revelation 12:11* – Overcome by the blood and testimony

Key Insight

The Word of God in your mouth is as powerful as the Word in God's mouth — when spoken in faith.

Reflection Journal

- Do I know my spiritual rights as a believer?
- What scriptures am I actively standing on today?
- Have I allowed fear or ignorance to silence my authority?

Prayer of Empowerment

Father, open my eyes to the authority I have in Christ. Teach me to wield Your Word with boldness and faith. Where I have allowed fear or ignorance to reign, let revelation come. I stand today as a child of God, armed with the Sword of the Spirit. I will speak the Word. I will stand in victory. I will not fear the enemy — for greater is He who is in me. In Jesus' name. Amen.

DAY 1: BLOODLINES & GATES — BREAKING FAMILY CHAINS

"*Our fathers have sinned and are no more, and we bear their punishment.*"
— Lamentations 5:7

You may be saved, but your bloodline still has a history — and until the old covenants are broken, they continue to speak.

Across every continent, there are hidden altars, ancestral pacts, secret vows, and inherited iniquities that remain active until they are specifically addressed. What started with great-grandparents may still be claiming the destinies of today's children.

Global Expressions

- **Africa** – Family gods, oracles, generational witchcraft, blood sacrifices.
- **Asia** – Ancestor worship, reincarnation bonds, karma chains.
- **Latin America** – Santeria, death altars, shamanistic blood oaths.
- **Europe** – Freemasonry, pagan roots, bloodline pacts.
- **North America** – New age inheritances, masonic lineage, occult objects.

The curse continues until someone rises to say, "No more!"

A Deeper Testimony – Healing from the Roots

A woman from West Africa, after reading *Greater Exploits 14*, realized her chronic miscarriages and unexplained torment were linked to her grandfather's position as a shrine priest. She had accepted Christ years ago but never dealt with the family covenants.

After three days of prayer and fasting, she was led to destroy certain heirlooms and renounce covenants using Galatians 3:13. That very month, she conceived and carried a child full term. Today, she leads others in healing and deliverance ministry.

Another man in Latin America, from the book *Delivered from the Power of Darkness*, found freedom after renouncing a Freemasonry curse that was secretly passed down from his great-grandfather. As he began applying scriptures like Isaiah 49:24–26 and engaging in deliverance prayers, his mental torment stopped and peace was restored in his home.

These stories are not coincidences — they are testimonies of truth in action.

Action Plan – Family Inventory

1. Write down all known family beliefs, practices, and affiliations — religious, mystical, or secret societies.
2. Ask God for revelation of hidden altars and pacts.
3. Prayerfully destroy and discard any object tied to idolatry or occult practices.
4. Fast as led and use the scriptures below to break legal ground:
   - *Leviticus 26:40–42*
   - *Isaiah 49:24–26*
   - *Galatians 3:13*

GROUP DISCUSSION & Application

- What common family practices are often overlooked as harmless but may be spiritually dangerous?
- Have members share anonymously (if needed) any dreams, objects, or recurring cycles in their bloodline.
- Group prayer of renunciation — each person can speak the name of the family or issue being renounced.

Ministry Tools: Bring anointing oil. Offer communion. Lead the group in a covenant prayer of replacement — dedicating each family line to Christ.

Key Insight

Being born again saves your spirit. Breaking family covenants preserves your destiny.

Reflection Journal

- What runs in my family? What needs to stop with me?
- Are there items, names, or traditions in my home that need to go?
- What doors did my forefathers open that I now need to shut?

Prayer of Release

Lord Jesus, I thank You for Your blood that speaks better things. Today I renounce every hidden altar, family covenant, and inherited bondage. I break the chains of my bloodline and declare that I am a new creation. My life, family, and destiny now belong to You alone. In Jesus' name. Amen.

DAY 2: DREAM INVASIONS — WHEN NIGHT BECOMES A BATTLEFIELD

"*While men slept, his enemy came and sowed tares among the wheat, and went his way.*" — Matthew 13:25

For many, the greatest spiritual warfare doesn't happen while awake — it happens when they are asleep.

Dreams are not just random brain activity. They are spiritual portals through which warnings, attacks, covenants, and destinies are exchanged. The enemy uses sleep as a silent battleground to sow fear, lust, confusion, and delay — all without resistance because most people are unaware of the warfare.

Global Expressions

- **Africa** – Spiritual spouses, serpents, eating in dreams, masquerades.
- **Asia** – Ancestral encounters, death dreams, karmic torment.
- **Latin America** – Animalistic demons, shadows, sleep paralysis.
- **North America** – Astral projection, alien dreams, trauma replays.
- **Europe** – Gothic manifestations, sex demons (incubus/succubus), soul fragmentations.

If Satan can control your dreams, he can influence your destiny.

Testimony – From Night Terror to Peace

A young woman from the United Kingdom emailed after reading *Ex-Satanist: The James Exchange*. She shared how for years, she'd been plagued by dreams of being chased, bitten by dogs, or sleeping with strange men — always followed by setbacks in real life. Her relationships failed, job opportunities evaporated, and she was constantly exhausted.

Through fasting and studying scriptures like Job 33:14–18, she discovered that God often speaks through dreams — but so does the enemy. She began to anoint her head with oil, reject evil dreams out loud upon waking, and keep a dream journal. Gradually, her dreams became clearer and peaceful. Today, she leads a support group for young women suffering from dream attacks.

A Nigerian businessman, after listening to a YouTube testimony, realized his dream of being served food every night was linked to witchcraft. Every time he accepted the food in his dream, things went wrong in his business. He learned to reject the food immediately in the dream, pray in tongues before bed, and now sees divine strategies and warnings instead.

Action Plan – Fortify Your Night Watches

1. **Before Bed:** Read scriptures out loud. Worship. Anoint your head with oil.
2. **Dream Journal:** Write down every dream upon waking — good or bad. Ask the Holy Spirit for interpretation.
3. **Reject & Renounce:** If the dream involves sexual activity, dead relatives, eating, or bondage — renounce it immediately in prayer.
4. **Scripture Warfare:**
    - *Psalm 4:8* — Peaceful sleep
    - *Job 33:14–18* — God speaks through dreams
    - *Matthew 13:25* — Enemy sowing tares
    - *Isaiah 54:17* — No weapon formed against you

Group Application

- Share recent dreams anonymously. Let the group discern patterns and meanings.
- Teach members how to reject evil dreams verbally and seal good ones in prayer.
- Group declaration: "We forbid demonic transactions in our dreams, in Jesus' name!"

Ministry Tools:

- Bring paper and pens for dream journaling.
- Demonstrate how to anoint one's home and bed.

- Offer communion as a covenant seal for the night.

Key Insight

Dreams are either gateways to divine encounters or demonic entrapments. Discernment is key.

Reflection Journal

- What kind of dreams have I consistently experienced?
- Do I take time to reflect on my dreams?
- Have my dreams been warning me about something I ignored?

Prayer of Night Watch

Father, I dedicate my dreams to You. Let no evil power project into my sleep. I reject every demonic covenant, sexual defilement, or manipulation in my dreams. I receive divine visitation, heavenly instruction, and angelic protection as I sleep. Let my nights be filled with peace, revelation, and power. In Jesus' name, amen.

DAY 3: SPIRITUAL SPOUSES — UNHOLY UNIONS THAT BIND DESTINIES

"*For your Maker is your husband—the Lord Almighty is His name...*" — Isaiah 54:5

"*They sacrificed their sons and their daughters unto devils.*" — Psalm 106:37

While many cry out for marital breakthrough, what they don't realize is that they're already in a **spiritual marriage** — one they never consented to.

These are **covenants formed through dreams, molestation, blood rituals, pornography, ancestral oaths, or demonic transfer**. The spirit spouse — incubus (male) or succubus (female) — takes on a legal right to the person's body, intimacy, and future, often blocking relationships, destroying homes, causing miscarriages, and fueling addictions.

Global Manifestations

- **Africa** – Marine spirits (Mami Wata), spirit wives/husbands from water kingdoms.
- **Asia** – Celestial marriages, karmic soulmate curses, reincarnated spouses.
- **Europe** – Witchcraft unions, demonic lovers from Freemasonry or Druid roots.
- **Latin America** – Santeria marriages, love spells, pact-based "spirit marriages."
- **North America** – Porn-induced spiritual portals, new age sex spirits, alien abductions as manifestations of incubus encounters.

Real Stories — The Battle for Marital Freedom
Tolu, Nigeria

Tolu was 32 and single. Every time she got engaged, the man would suddenly disappear. She constantly dreamed of being married in elaborate ceremonies. In *Greater Exploits 14*, she recognized her case matched a testimony shared there. She underwent a three-day fast and nightly warfare prayers at midnight, severing soul ties and casting out the marine spirit that claimed her. Today, she's married and counseling others.

Lina, Philippines

Lina often felt a "presence" lay with her at night. She thought she was imagining things until bruises began to appear on her legs and thighs with no explanation. Her pastor discerned a spiritual spouse. She confessed a past abortion and pornography addiction, then underwent deliverance. She now helps young women identify similar patterns in her community.

Action Plan – Breaking the Covenant

1. **Confess** and repent of sexual sins, soul ties, occult exposure, or ancestral rituals.
2. **Reject** all spiritual marriages in prayer — by name, if revealed.
3. **Fast** for 3 days (or as led) with Isaiah 54 and Psalm 18 as anchor scriptures.
4. **Destroy** physical tokens: rings, clothes, or gifts tied to past lovers or occult affiliations.
5. **Declare out loud**:

I am not married to any spirit. I am covenanted to Jesus Christ. I reject every demonic union in my body, soul, and spirit!

Scripture Tools

- Isaiah 54:4–8 – God as your true Husband
- Psalm 18 – Breaking cords of death
- 1 Corinthians 6:15–20 – Your body belongs to the Lord
- Hosea 2:6–8 – Breaking ungodly covenants

Group Application

- Ask group members: Have you ever had dreams of weddings, sex with

strangers, or shadowy figures at night?
- Lead a group renunciation of spiritual spouses.
- Roleplay a "divorce court in heaven" — each participant files a spiritual divorce before God in prayer.
- Use anointing oil on the head, belly, and feet as symbols of cleansing, reproduction, and movement.

Key Insight

Demonic marriages are real. But there is no spiritual union that cannot be broken by the blood of Jesus.

Reflection Journal

- Have I had recurring dreams of marriage or sex?
- Are there patterns of rejection, delay, or miscarriage in my life?
- Am I willing to fully surrender my body, sexuality, and future to God?

Prayer of Deliverance

Heavenly Father, I repent of every sexual sin, known or unknown. I reject and renounce every spiritual spouse, marine spirit, or occult marriage claiming my life. By the power in the blood of Jesus, I break every covenant, dream seed, and soul tie. I declare I am the Bride of Christ, set apart for His glory. I walk free, in Jesus' name. Amen.

DAY 4: CURSED OBJECTS – DOORS THAT DEFILE

"**N**either shall you bring an abomination into your house, lest you be cursed like it." — Deuteronomy 7:26

A Hidden Entry Many Ignore

Not every possession is just a possession. Some things carry history. Others carry spirits. Cursed objects are not only idols or artifacts — they can be books, jewelry, statues, symbols, gifts, clothes, or even inherited heirlooms that were once dedicated to dark forces. What's on your shelf, your wrist, your wall — may be the very point of entry for torment in your life.

Global Observations

- **Africa**: Calabashes, charms, and bracelets tied to witch doctors or ancestral worship.
- **Asia**: Amulets, zodiac statues, and temple souvenirs.
- **Latin America**: Santería necklaces, dolls, candles with spirit inscriptions.
- **North America**: Tarot cards, Ouija boards, dream catchers, horror memorabilia.
- **Europe**: Pagan relics, occult books, witch-themed accessories.

A couple in Europe experienced sudden sickness and spiritual oppression after returning from vacation in Bali. Unaware, they had bought a carved statue that had been dedicated to a local sea deity. After prayer and discernment, they removed the item and burned it. Peace returned immediately.

Another woman from the *Greater Exploits* testimonies reported unexplainable nightmares, until it was revealed that a gifted necklace from her aunt was actually a spiritual monitoring device consecrated in a shrine.

You don't just clean your house physically — you must also clean it spiritually.

Testimony: "The Doll That Watched Me"

Lourdes Valdivia, whose story we explored earlier from South America, once received a porcelain doll during a family celebration. Her mother had consecrated it in an occult ritual. From the night it was brought into her room, Lourdes began hearing voices, experiencing sleep paralysis, and seeing figures at night.

It wasn't until a Christian friend prayed with her and the Holy Spirit revealed the doll's origin that she got rid of it. Immediately, the demonic presence left. This began her awakening — from oppression to deliverance.

Action Plan – House & Heart Audit

1. **Walk through every room** in your home with anointing oil and the Word.
2. **Ask the Holy Spirit** to highlight objects or gifts that are not of God.
3. **Burn or discard** items that are linked to the occult, idolatry, or immorality.
4. **Close all doors** with scriptures like:
    - *Deuteronomy 7:26*
    - *Acts 19:19*
    - *2 Corinthians 6:16–18*

Group Discussion & Activation

- Share any items or gifts you once owned that had unusual effects in your life.
- Create a "House Cleansing Checklist" together.
- Assign partners to pray through each other's home environments (with permission).
- Invite a local deliverance minister to lead a prophetic home-cleansing prayer.

Tools for Ministry: Anointing oil, worship music, trash bags (for real discarding), and a fire-safe container for items to be destroyed.

Key Insight
What you permit in your space can authorize spirits in your life.

Reflection Journal

- What items in my home or wardrobe have unclear spiritual origins?
- Have I held onto something because of sentimental value that I now need to let go?
- Am I ready to sanctify my space for the Holy Spirit?

Prayer of Cleansing

Lord Jesus, I invite Your Holy Spirit to expose anything in my home that is not of You. I renounce every cursed object, gift, or item that was tied to darkness. I declare my home holy ground. Let Your peace and purity dwell here. In Jesus' name. Amen.

DAY 5: CHARMED & DECEIVED — BREAKING FREE FROM THE SPIRIT OF DIVINATION

"These men are servants of the Most High God, who proclaim to us the way of salvation." — *Acts 16:17 (NKJV)*

"But Paul, greatly annoyed, turned and said to the spirit, 'I command you in the name of Jesus Christ to come out of her.' And he came out that very hour." — *Acts 16:18*

There's a thin line between prophecy and divination — and many today are crossing it without even knowing.

From YouTube prophets charging for "personal words," to social media tarot readers quoting scriptures, the world has become a marketplace of spiritual noise. And tragically, many believers are unknowingly drinking from polluted streams.

The **spirit of divination** mimics the Holy Spirit. It flatters, seduces, manipulates emotions, and ensnares its victims in a web of control. Its goal? **To spiritually entangle, deceive, and enslave.**

Global Expressions of Divination

- **Africa** – Oracles, Ifá priests, water spirit mediums, prophetic fraud.
- **Asia** – Palm readers, astrologers, ancestral seers, reincarnation "prophets."
- **Latin America** – Santeria prophets, charm-makers, saints with dark powers.
- **Europe** – Tarot cards, clairvoyance, medium circles, New Age channeling.
- **North America** – "Christian" psychics, numerology in churches, angel cards, spirit guides disguised as Holy Spirit.

What's dangerous is not just what they say — but the **spirit** behind it.

Testimony: From Clairvoyant to Christ

An American woman testified on YouTube how she went from being a "Christian prophetess" to realizing she was operating under a spirit of divination. She began seeing visions clearly, giving detailed prophetic words, and drawing large crowds online. But she also battled depression, nightmares, and heard whispering voices after every session.

One day, while watching a teaching on *Acts 16*, the scales fell off. She realized she had never submitted to the Holy Spirit — only to her gift. After deep repentance and deliverance, she destroyed her angel cards and fasting journal filled with rituals. Today, she preaches Jesus, no longer "words."

Action Plan – Testing the Spirits

1. Ask: Does this word/gift draw me to **Christ**, or to the **person** giving it?
2. Test every spirit with *1 John 4:1–3*.
3. Repent for any involvement with psychic, occult, or counterfeit prophetic practices.
4. Break all soul ties with false prophets, diviners, or witchcraft instructors (even online).
5. Declare with boldness:

"I reject every lying spirit. I belong to Jesus alone. My ears are tuned to His voice!"

Group Application

- Discuss: Have you ever followed a prophet or spiritual guide that later turned out false?
- Group Exercise: Lead members to renounce specific practices like astrology, soul readings, psychic games, or spiritual influencers not rooted in Christ.
- Invite the Holy Spirit: Allow 10 minutes for silence and listening. Then share what God reveals — if anything.
- Burn or delete digital/physical items related to divination, including books, apps, videos, or notes.

Ministry Tools:

Deliverance oil, cross (symbol of submission), bin/bucket for discarding symbolic items, worship music centered on the Holy Spirit.

Key Insight

Not all supernatural is from God. True prophecy flows from intimacy with Christ, not manipulation or spectacle.

Reflection Journal

- Have I ever been drawn to psychic or manipulative spiritual practices?
- Am I more addicted to "words" than the Word of God?
- What voices have I given access to that now need to be silenced?

PRAYER OF DELIVERANCE

Father, I come out of agreement with every spirit of divination, manipulation, and counterfeit prophecy. I repent for seeking direction apart from Your voice. Cleanse my mind, my soul, and my spirit. Teach me to walk by Your Spirit alone. I close every door I opened to the occult, knowingly or unknowingly. I declare that Jesus is my Shepherd, and I hear only His voice. In Jesus' mighty name, Amen.

DAY 6: GATES OF THE EYE – SHUTTING DOWN PORTALS OF DARKNESS

"The eye is the lamp of the body. If your eyes are healthy, your whole body will be full of light."
— *Matthew 6:22 (NIV)*

"I will set no wicked thing before mine eyes..." — *Psalm 101:3 (KJV)*

In the spiritual realm, **your eyes are gates.** What enters through your eyes affects your soul — for purity or pollution. The enemy knows this. That's why media, images, pornography, horror movies, occult symbols, fashion trends, and seductive content have become battlegrounds.

The war for your attention is a war for your soul.

What many consider "harmless entertainment" is often a coded invitation — to lust, fear, manipulation, pride, vanity, rebellion, or even demonic attachment.

Global Gateways of Visual Darkness

- **Africa** – Ritual movies, Nollywood themes normalizing witchcraft and polygamy.
- **Asia** – Anime and manga with spiritual portals, seductive spirits, astral travel.
- **Europe** – Gothic fashion, horror films, vampire obsessions, satanic art.
- **Latin America** – Telenovelas glorifying sorcery, curses, and revenge.
- **North America** – Mainstream media, music videos, pornography, "cute" demonic cartoons.

What you consistently gaze upon, you become desensitized to.

Story: "The Cartoon That Cursed My Child"

A mother from the U.S. noticed her 5-year-old began screaming at night and drawing disturbing images. After prayer, the Holy Spirit pointed her to a cartoon her son had been watching secretly — one filled with spells, talking spirits, and symbols she hadn't noticed.

She deleted the shows and anointed her house and screens. After several nights of midnight prayer and Psalm 91, the attacks ceased, and the boy began sleeping peacefully. She now leads a support group helping parents guard their children's visual gates.

Action Plan – Purifying the Eye Gate

1. Do a **media audit**: What are you watching? Reading? Scrolling?
2. Cancel subscriptions or platforms that feed your flesh instead of your faith.
3. Anoint your eyes and screens, declaring Psalm 101:3.
4. Replace garbage with godly input — documentaries, worship, pure entertainment.
5. Declare:

"I will set no vile thing before my eyes. My vision belongs to God."

Group Application

- Challenge: 7-Day Eye Gate Fast — no toxic media, no idle scrolling.
- Share: What content has the Holy Spirit told you to stop watching?
- Exercise: Lay hands on your eyes and renounce any defilement through vision (e.g., pornography, horror, vanity).
- Activity: Invite members to delete apps, burn books, or discard items that corrupt their sight.

Tools: Olive oil, accountability apps, scripture screensavers, eye gate prayer cards.

Key Insight

You cannot walk in authority over demons if you are entertained by them.

Reflection Journal

- What do I feed my eyes that may be feeding darkness in my life?
- When did I last weep over what breaks God's heart?
- Have I given the Holy Spirit full control over my screen time?

Prayer of Purity

Lord Jesus, I ask for Your blood to wash over my eyes. Forgive me for the things I've allowed in through my screens, books, and imaginations. Today, I declare my eyes are for light, not darkness. I reject every image, lust, and influence not from You. Purify my soul. Guard my gaze. And let me see what You see — in holiness and truth. Amen.

DAY 7: THE POWER BEHIND NAMES — RENOUNCING UNHOLY IDENTITIES

"And Jabez called on the God of Israel saying, 'Oh that You would bless me indeed...' So God granted him what he requested."
— *1 Chronicles 4:10*

"You shall no longer be called Abram, but Abraham..." — *Genesis 17:5*

Names are not just labels — they are spiritual declarations. In scripture, names often reflected destiny, personality, or even bondage. To name something is to give it identity and direction. The enemy understands this — that's why many people are unknowingly trapped under names given in ignorance, pain, or spiritual bondage.

Just as God changed names (Abram to Abraham, Jacob to Israel, Sarai to Sarah), He still changes destinies by renaming His people.

Global Contexts of Name Bondage

- **Africa** – Children named after dead ancestors or idols ("Ogbanje," "Dike," "Ifunanya" tied to meanings).
- **Asia** – Reincarnation names tied to karmic cycles or deities.
- **Europe** – Names rooted in pagan or witchcraft heritage (e.g., Freya, Thor, Merlin).
- **Latin America** – Santeria-influenced names, especially through spiritual baptisms.
- **North America** – Names taken from pop culture, rebellion movements, or ancestral dedications.

Names matter — and they can carry power, blessing, or bondage.

Story: "Why I Had to Rename My Daughter"

In *Greater Exploits 14*, a Nigerian couple named their daughter "Amaka," meaning "beautiful," but she suffered a rare illness that baffled doctors. During a prophetic conference, the mother received revelation: the name was once used by her grandmother, a witch doctor, whose spirit was now claiming the child.

They changed her name to "Oluwatamilore" (God has blessed me), followed with fasting and prayers. The child recovered fully.

Another case from India involved a man named "Karma," struggling with generational curses. After renouncing Hindu ties and changing his name to "Jonathan," he began experiencing breakthrough in finances and health.

Action Plan – Investigating Your Name

1. Research the full meaning of your names — first, middle, surname.
2. Ask parents or elders why you were given those names.
3. Renounce negative spiritual meanings or dedications in prayer.
4. Declare your divine identity in Christ:

"I am called by God's name. My new name is written in heaven (Revelation 2:17)."

GROUP ENGAGEMENT

- Ask members: What does your name mean? Have you had dreams involving it?
- Do a "naming prayer" — prophetically declaring each person's identity.
- Lay hands on those who need to break from names tied to covenants or ancestral bondage.

Tools: Print name meaning cards, bring anointing oil, use scriptures of name changes.

Key Insight
You can't walk in your true identity while still answering to a false one.

Reflection Journal

- What does my name mean — spiritually and culturally?
- Do I feel aligned with my name or in conflict with it?
- What name does heaven call me?

Prayer of Renaming

Father, in the name of Jesus, I thank You for giving me a new identity in Christ. I break every curse, covenant, or demonic tie connected to my names. I renounce every name that does not align with Your will. I receive the name and identity heaven has given me — full of power, purpose, and purity. In Jesus' name, Amen.

DAY 8: UNMASKING FALSE LIGHT — NEW AGE TRAPS AND ANGELIC DECEPTIONS

"And no wonder! For Satan himself transforms himself into an angel of light." — 2 Corinthians 11:14

"Beloved, do not believe every spirit, but test the spirits to see whether they are from God..." — 1 John 4:1

Not all that glows is God.

In today's world, a growing number of people seek "light," "healing," and "energy" outside the Word of God. They turn to meditation, yoga altars, third-eye activations, ancestral summoning, tarot readings, moon rituals, angelic channeling, and even Christian-sounding mysticism. The deception is strong because it often comes with peace, beauty, and power — at first.

But behind these movements are spirits of divination, false prophecy, and ancient deities who wear the mask of light to gain legal access to people's souls.

Global Reach of False Light

- **North America** – Crystals, sage cleansing, law of attraction, psychics, alien light codes.
- **Europe** – Rebranded paganism, goddess worship, white witchcraft, spiritual festivals.
- **Latin America** – Santeria blended with Catholic saints, spiritist healers (curanderos).
- **Africa** – Prophetic counterfeits using angel altars and ritual water.
- **Asia** – Chakras, yoga "enlightenment," reincarnation counseling, temple spirits.

These practices may offer temporary "light," but they darken the soul over time.

Testimony: Deliverance from the Light That Deceived

From *Greater Exploits 14*, Mercy (UK) had been attending angel workshops and practicing "Christian" meditation with incense, crystals, and angel cards. She believed she was accessing God's light, but soon began hearing voices during her sleep and feeling unexplained fear at night.

Her deliverance began when someone gifted her *The Jameses Exchange*, and she realized the similarities between her experiences and that of an ex-satanist who spoke of angelic deceptions. She repented, destroyed all occult objects, and submitted to full deliverance prayers.

Today, she testifies boldly against New Age deception in churches and has helped others renounce similar paths.

Action Plan – Testing the Spirits

1. **Inventory your practices and beliefs** — Do they line up with Scripture or just feel spiritual?
2. **Renounce and destroy** all false-light materials: crystals, yoga manuals, angel cards, dreamcatchers, etc.
3. **Pray Psalm 119:105** — ask God to make His Word your only light.
4. **Declare war on confusion** — bind familiar spirits and false revelation.

GROUP APPLICATION

- **Discuss**: Have you or someone you know been drawn into "spiritual" practices that didn't center on Jesus?
- **Roleplay Discernment**: Read excerpts of "spiritual" sayings (e.g., "Trust the universe") and contrast them with Scripture.
- **Anointing & Deliverance Session**: Break altars to false light and replace with covenant to the *Light of the World* (John 8:12).

Ministry Tools:

- Bring actual New Age items (or photos of them) for object-teaching.
- Offer deliverance prayer against familiar spirits (see Acts 16:16–18).

Key Insight
Satan's most dangerous weapon isn't darkness — it's counterfeit light.

Reflection Journal

- Have I opened spiritual doors through "light" teachings not rooted in Scripture?
- Do I trust in the Holy Spirit or in intuition and energy?
- Am I willing to surrender all forms of false spirituality for God's truth?

PRAYER OF RENUNCIATION

Father, I repent for every way I have entertained or engaged with the false light. I renounce all forms of New Age, witchcraft, and deceptive spirituality. I break every soul tie to angelic imposters, spirit guides, and false revelation. I receive Jesus, the true Light of the world. I declare I will follow no voice but Yours, in Jesus' name. Amen.

DAY 9: THE ALTAR OF BLOOD — COVENANTS THAT DEMAND A LIFE

"*And they built the high places of Baal... to cause their sons and their daughters to pass through the fire unto Molech.*" — Jeremiah 32:35

"*And they overcame him by the blood of the Lamb and by the word of their testimony...*" — Revelation 12:11

There are altars that don't just request your attention — they demand your blood.

From ancient times to the present day, blood covenants have been a core practice of the kingdom of darkness. Some are entered into knowingly through witchcraft, abortion, ritual killings, or occult initiations. Others are inherited through ancestral practices or unknowingly joined through spiritual ignorance.

Wherever innocent blood is shed — whether in shrines, bedrooms, or boardrooms — a demonic altar speaks.

These altars claim lives, cut short destinies, and create a legal ground for demonic affliction.

Global Altars of Blood

- **Africa** – Ritual killings, money rituals, child sacrifices, blood pacts at birth.
- **Asia** – Temple blood offerings, family curses through abortion or war oaths.
- **Latin America** – Santeria animal sacrifices, blood offerings to spirits of the dead.
- **North America** – Abortion-as-sacrament ideology, demonic blood oath fraternities.
- **Europe** – Ancient Druid and Freemason rites, WW-era bloodshed altars still unrepented.

These covenants, unless broken, continue to claim lives, often in cycles.

True Story: A Father's Sacrifice

In *Delivered from the Power of Darkness*, a woman from Central Africa discovered during a deliverance session that her frequent brushes with death were connected to a blood oath her father had made. He had promised her life in exchange for wealth after years of infertility.

After her father died, she began seeing shadows and experiencing near-fatal accidents every year on her birthday. Her breakthrough came when she was led to declare Psalm 118:17 — *"I shall not die but live..."* — over herself daily, followed by a series of renunciation prayers and fasting. Today, she leads a powerful intercessory ministry.

Another account from *Greater Exploits 14* describes a man in Latin America who participated in a gang initiation that involved shedding blood. Years later, even after accepting Christ, his life was in constant turmoil — until he broke the blood covenant through an extended fast, public confession, and water baptism. The torment stopped.

Action Plan – Silencing the Blood Altars

1. **Repent** for any abortion, occult blood pacts, or inherited bloodshed.
2. **Renounce** all known and unknown blood covenants aloud by name.
3. **Fast for 3 days** with communion taken daily, declaring the blood of Jesus as your legal covering.
4. **Declare aloud**:

"By the blood of Jesus, I break every blood covenant made on my behalf. I am redeemed!"

GROUP APPLICATION

- Discuss the difference between natural blood ties and demonic blood covenants.
- Use red ribbon/thread to represent blood altars, and scissors to cut them prophetically.
- Invite a testimony from someone who has broken free from blood-

linked bondage.

Ministry Tools:

- Communion elements
- Anointing oil
- Deliverance declarations
- Candlelight altar-breaking visual if possible

Key Insight
Satan trades in blood. Jesus overpaid for your freedom with His.

Reflection Journal

- Have I or my family participated in anything that involved bloodshed or oaths?
- Are there recurring deaths, miscarriages, or violent patterns in my bloodline?
- Have I fully trusted the blood of Jesus to speak louder over my life?

Prayer of Deliverance

Lord Jesus, I thank You for Your precious blood that speaks better things than the blood of Abel. I repent for any covenant of blood that I or my ancestors made, knowingly or unknowingly. I renounce them now. I declare that I am covered by the blood of the Lamb. Let every demonic altar demanding my life be silenced and shattered. I live because You died for me. In Jesus' name, Amen.

DAY 10: BARRENNESS & BROKENNESS — WHEN THE WOMB BECOMES A BATTLEFIELD

"None shall miscarry or be barren in your land; I will fulfill the number of your days." — Exodus 23:26

"He gives the childless woman a family, making her a happy mother. Praise the Lord!" — Psalm 113:9

Infertility is more than a medical issue. It can be a spiritual stronghold rooted in deep emotional, ancestral, and even territorial battles.

Across nations, barrenness is used by the enemy to shame, isolate, and destroy women and families. While some causes are physiological, many are deeply spiritual — tied to generational altars, curses, spirit spouses, aborted destinies, or soul wounds.

Behind every unfruitful womb, heaven has a promise. But there is often a warfare that must be waged before conception — in the womb and in the spirit.

Global Patterns of Barrenness

- **Africa** – Linked to polygamy, ancestral curses, shrine pacts, and spirit children.
- **Asia** – Karma beliefs, past-life vows, generational curses, shame culture.
- **Latin America** – Witchcraft-induced womb closure, envy spells.
- **Europe** – IVF overdependence, Freemasonry child sacrifices, abortion guilt.
- **North America** – Emotional trauma, soul wounds, miscarriage cycles, hormone-altering meds.

REAL STORIES – FROM Tears to Testimonies

Maria from Bolivia (Latin America)

Maria had suffered 5 miscarriages. Each time, she would dream of holding a crying baby and then see blood the next morning. Doctors could not explain her condition. After reading a testimony in *Greater Exploits*, she realized she had inherited a family altar of barrenness from a grandmother who had dedicated all female wombs to a local deity.

She fasted and declared Psalm 113 for 14 days. Her pastor led her in breaking the covenant using communion. Nine months later, she gave birth to twins.

Ngozi from Nigeria (Africa)

Ngozi had been married for 10 years without a child. During deliverance prayers, it was revealed that she had been married in the spirit realm to a marine husband. Every ovulation cycle, she'd have sexual dreams. After a series of midnight warfare prayers, and a prophetic act of burning her wedding ring from a past occult initiation, her womb opened.

Action Plan – Opening the Womb

1. **Identify the root** – ancestral, emotional, marital, or medical.
2. **Repent of past abortions**, soul ties, sexual sins, and occult dedications.
3. **Anoint your womb daily** while declaring Exodus 23:26 and Psalm 113.
4. **Fast for 3 days**, and take communion daily, rejecting all altars tied to your womb.
5. **Speak aloud**:

My womb is blessed. I reject every covenant of barrenness. I shall conceive and carry to full term by the power of the Holy Spirit!

Group Application

- Invite women (and couples) to share burdens of delay in a safe, prayerful space.
- Use red scarves or cloths tied around the waist — then prophetically untied as a sign of freedom.
- Lead a prophetic "naming" ceremony — declare children yet to be born by faith.
- Break word curses, cultural shame, and self-hate in prayer circles.

Ministry Tools:

- Olive oil (anoint wombs)
- Communion
- Mantles/shawls (symbolizing covering and newness)

Key Insight

Barrenness is not the end — it is a call to war, to faith, and to restoration. God's delay is not denial.

Reflection Journal

- What emotional or spiritual wounds are tied to my womb?
- Have I allowed shame or bitterness to replace my hope?
- Am I willing to confront the root causes with faith and action?

Prayer of Healing & Conception

Father, I stand on Your Word that says none shall be barren in the land. I reject every lie, altar, and spirit assigned to block my fruitfulness. I forgive myself and others who have spoken evil over my body. I receive healing, restoration, and life. I declare my womb fruitful, and my joy full. In Jesus' name. Amen.

DAY 11: AUTOIMMUNE DISORDERS & CHRONIC FATIGUE — THE INVISIBLE WAR WITHIN

"*A house divided against itself shall not stand.*" — Matthew 12:25
"*He gives power to the weak, and to those who have no might He increases strength.*" — Isaiah 40:29

Autoimmune diseases are where the body attacks itself — mistaking its own cells as enemies. Lupus, rheumatoid arthritis, multiple sclerosis, Hashimoto's, and others fall under this group.

Chronic fatigue syndrome (CFS), fibromyalgia, and other unexplained exhaustion disorders often overlap with autoimmune struggles. But beyond the biological, many who suffer carry emotional trauma, soul wounds, and spiritual burdens.

The body is crying out — not just for medication, but for peace. Many are at war within.

Global Glimpse

- **Africa** – Increasing autoimmune diagnoses linked with trauma, pollution, and stress.
- **Asia** – High rates of thyroid disorders linked to ancestral suppression and shame culture.
- **Europe & America** – Chronic fatigue and burnout epidemic from performance-driven culture.
- **Latin America** – Sufferers often misdiagnosed; stigma and spiritual attacks through soul fragmentation or curses.

Hidden Spiritual Roots

- **Self-hatred or shame** — feeling "not good enough."
- **Unforgiveness toward self or others** — the immune system mimics the spiritual condition.
- **Unprocessed grief or betrayal** — opens the door to soul fatigue and physical breakdown.
- **Witchcraft affliction or jealousy arrows** — used to drain spiritual and physical strength.

True Stories – Battles Fought in the Dark
Elena from Spain

Elena was diagnosed with lupus after a long abusive relationship that left her emotionally broken. In therapy and prayer, it was revealed that she had internalized hatred, believing she was worthless. When she began to forgive herself and confront soul wounds with Scripture, her flare-ups reduced drastically. She testifies to the healing power of the Word and soul cleansing.

James from the U.S.

James, a driven corporate executive, collapsed from CFS after 20 years of non-stop stress. During deliverance, it was exposed that a generational curse of striving without rest plagued the men in his family. He entered a season of sabbath, prayer, and confession, and found restoration not just of health, but of identity.

Action Plan – Healing the Soul and Immune System

1. **Pray Psalm 103:1–5** aloud every morning — especially v.3-5.
2. **List your inner beliefs** — what do you say to yourself? Break lies.
3. **Forgive deeply** — especially yourself.
4. **Take communion** to reset body covenant — see Isaiah 53.
5. **Rest in God** — Sabbath isn't optional, it's spiritual warfare against burnout.

I declare my body is not my enemy. Every cell in me shall align with divine order and peace. I receive God's strength and healing.

Group Application

- Have members share fatigue patterns or emotional exhaustion they

hide.
- Do a "soul dump" exercise — writing down burdens, then burn or bury them symbolically.
- Lay hands on those suffering autoimmune symptoms; command balance and peace.
- Encourage 7-day journaling of emotional triggers and healing Scriptures.

Ministry Tools:

- Essential oils or fragrant anointing for refreshment
- Journals or notepads
- Psalm 23 meditation soundtrack

Key Insight
What attacks the soul often manifests in the body. Healing must flow from the inside out.

Reflection Journal

- Do I feel safe in my own body and thoughts?
- Am I harboring shame or blame from past failures or trauma?
- What can I do to start honoring rest and peace as spiritual practices?

Prayer of Restoration
Lord Jesus, You are my Healer. Today I reject every lie that I am broken, dirty, or doomed. I forgive myself and others. I bless every cell in my body. I receive peace in my soul and alignment in my immune system. By Your stripes, I am healed. Amen.

DAY 12: EPILEPSY & MENTAL TORMENT — WHEN THE MIND BECOMES A BATTLEGROUND

"*Lord, have mercy on my son: for he is lunatick, and sore vexed: for ofttimes he falleth into the fire, and oft into the water.*" — Matthew 17:15

"*God has not given us a spirit of fear, but of power, love, and a sound mind.*" — 2 Timothy 1:7

Some afflictions are not just medical — they are spiritual battlegrounds disguised as sickness.

Epilepsy, seizures, schizophrenia, bipolar episodes, and patterns of torment in the mind often have unseen roots. While medication has a place, discernment is critical. In many biblical accounts, seizures and mental attacks were the result of demonic oppression.

Modern society medicates what Jesus often *cast out*.

Global Reality

- **Africa** – Seizures frequently attributed to curses or ancestral spirits.
- **Asia** – Epileptics often hidden due to shame and spiritual stigma.
- **Latin America** – Schizophrenia linked with generational witchcraft or aborted callings.
- **Europe & North America** – Overdiagnosis and overmedication often mask demonic root causes.

Real Stories – Deliverance in the Fire
Musa from Northern Nigeria

Musa had epileptic seizures since childhood. His family tried everything — from native doctors to church prayers. One day, during a deliverance service, the Spirit revealed that Musa's grandfather had offered him in a witchcraft exchange. After breaking the covenant and anointing him, he never had another seizure.

Daniel from Peru

Diagnosed with bipolar disorder, Daniel struggled with violent dreams and voices. He later discovered his father had been involved in secret satanic rituals in the mountains. Deliverance prayers and a three-day fast brought clarity. The voices stopped. Today, Daniel is calm, restored, and preparing for ministry.

Signs to Watch

- Repeated episodes of seizure without known neurological cause.
- Voices, hallucinations, violent or suicidal thoughts.
- Loss of time or memory, unexplainable fear, or physical fits during prayer.
- Family patterns of insanity or suicide.

Action Plan – Taking Authority Over the Mind

1. **Repent of all known occult ties, trauma, or curses.**
2. **Lay hands on your head daily, declaring a sound mind (2 Timothy 1:7).**
3. **Fast and pray over mind-binding spirits.**
4. **Break ancestral oaths, dedications, or bloodline curses.**
5. **If possible, join with a strong prayer partner or deliverance team.**

I reject every spirit of torment, seizure, and confusion. I receive a sound mind and stable emotions in Jesus' name!

Group Ministry & Application

- Identify family patterns of mental illness or seizures.
- Pray over those suffering — use anointing oil on the forehead.

- Have intercessors walk around the room declaring "Peace, be still!" (Mark 4:39)
- Invite those affected to break verbal agreements: "I am not insane. I am healed and whole."

Ministry Tools:

- Anointing oil
- Healing declaration cards
- Worship music that ministers peace and identity

Key Insight

Not every affliction is just physical. Some are rooted in ancient covenants and demonic legal grounds that must be addressed spiritually.

Reflection Journal

- Have I ever been tormented in my thoughts or sleep?
- Are there unhealed traumas or spiritual doors I need to shut?
- What truth can I declare daily to anchor my mind in God's Word?

Prayer of Soundness

Lord Jesus, You are the Restorer of my mind. I renounce every covenant, trauma, or demonic spirit attacking my brain, emotions, and clarity. I receive healing and a sound mind. I decree I will live, and not die. I will function in full strength, in Jesus' name. Amen.

DAY 13: SPIRIT OF FEAR — BREAKING THE CAGE OF INVISIBLE TORMENT

"*For God hath not given us the spirit of fear; but of power, and of love, and of a sound mind.*" — 2 Timothy 1:7
"*Fear hath torment...*" — 1 John 4:18

Fear is not just an emotion — it can be a *spirit*.

It whispers failure before you start. It magnifies rejection. It cripples purpose. It paralyzes nations.

Many are in invisible prisons built by fear: fear of death, failure, poverty, people, sickness, spiritual warfare, and the unknown.

Behind many anxiety attacks, panic disorders, and irrational phobias lies a spiritual assignment sent to **neutralize destinies**.

Global Manifestations

- **Africa** – Fear rooted in generational curses, ancestral retaliation, or witchcraft backlash.
- **Asia** – Cultural shame, karmic fear, reincarnation anxieties.
- **Latin America** – Fear from curses, village legends, and spiritual retaliation.
- **Europe & North America** – Hidden anxiety, diagnosed disorders, fear of confrontation, success, or rejection — often spiritual but labeled psychological.

Real Stories – Unmasking the Spirit
Sarah from Canada

For years, Sarah couldn't sleep in darkness. She always felt a presence in the room. Doctors diagnosed it as anxiety, but no treatment worked. During an online deliverance session, it was revealed that a childhood fear opened a door to a tormenting spirit through a nightmare and horror movie. She repented, renounced the fear, and commanded it to go. She now sleeps in peace.

Uche from Nigeria

Uche was called to preach but every time he stood before people, he froze. The fear was unnatural — choking, paralyzing. In prayer, God showed him a word curse spoken by a teacher who mocked his voice as a child. That word formed a spiritual chain. Once broken, he began preaching with boldness.

Action Plan – Overcoming Fear

1. **Confess any fear by name**: "I renounce the fear of [_____] in Jesus' name."
2. **Read aloud Psalm 27 and Isaiah 41 daily.**
3. **Worship until peace replaces panic.**
4. **Fast from fear-based media — horror movies, news, gossip.**
5. **Declare daily**: "I have a sound mind. I am not a slave to fear."

Group Application – Community Breakthrough

- Ask group members: What fear has paralyzed you the most?
- Break into small groups and lead prayers of **renunciation** and **replacement** (e.g., fear → boldness, anxiety → confidence).
- Have each person write down a fear and burn it as a prophetic act.
- Use *anointing oil* and *scripture confessions* over each other.

Ministry Tools:

- Anointing oil
- Scripture declaration cards
- Worship song: "No Longer Slaves" by Bethel

Key Insight

Fear tolerated is **faith contaminated**.
You cannot be bold and fearful at the same time — choose boldness.

Reflection Journal

- What fear has stayed with me since childhood?
- How has fear affected my decisions, health, or relationships?
- What would I do differently if I were completely free?

Prayer of Freedom from Fear

Father, I renounce the spirit of fear. I close every door through trauma, words, or sin that gave fear access. I receive the Spirit of power, love, and a sound mind. I declare boldness, peace, and victory in Jesus' name. Fear has no more place in my life. Amen.

DAY 14: SATANIC MARKINGS — ERASING THE UNHOLY BRAND

"*From henceforth let no man trouble me: for I bear in my body the marks of the Lord Jesus.*" — Galatians 6:17

"*They shall put my name upon the children of Israel; and I will bless them.*" — Numbers 6:27

Many destinies are silently *marked* in the spiritual realm — not by God, but by the enemy.

These satanic markings may come in the form of strange body signs, dreams of tattoos or branding, traumatic abuse, blood rituals, or inherited altars. Some are invisible — only discerned through spiritual sensitivity — while others show up as physical signs, demonic tattoos, spiritual branding, or persistent infirmities.

When a person is marked by the enemy, they may experience:

- Constant rejection and hatred without cause.
- Repeated spiritual attacks and blockages.
- Premature death or health crises at certain ages.
- Being tracked in the spirit — always visible to darkness.

These marks operate as *legal tags*, giving dark spirits permission to torment, delay, or monitor.

But the blood of Jesus **cleanses** and **rebrands**.

Global Expressions

- **Africa** – Tribal markings, ritual cuts, occult initiation scars.
- **Asia** – Spiritual seals, ancestral symbols, karmic marks.
- **Latin America** – Brujeria (witchcraft) initiation marks, birth signs

used in rituals.
- **Europe** – Freemasonry emblems, tattoos invoking spirit guides.
- **North America** – New age symbols, ritual abuse tattoos, demonic branding through occult covenants.

Real Stories – The Power of Rebranding
David from Uganda
David constantly faced rejection. No one could explain why, despite his talent. In prayer, a prophet saw a "spiritual X" on his forehead — a mark from a childhood ritual done by a village priest. During deliverance, the mark was spiritually erased through anointing oil and blood-of-Jesus declarations. His life shifted within weeks — he got married, landed a job, and became a youth leader.

Sandra from Brazil
Sandra had a dragon tattoo from her teenage rebellion. After giving her life to Christ, she noticed intense spiritual attacks whenever she fasted or prayed. Her pastor discerned the tattoo was a demonic symbol linked to monitoring spirits. After a session of repentance, prayer, and inner healing, she had the tattoo removed and broke the soul tie. Her nightmares stopped immediately.

Action Plan – Erase the Mark

1. **Ask the Holy Spirit** to reveal any spiritual or physical markings in your life.
2. **Repent** for any personal or inherited involvement in the rituals that allowed them.
3. **Apply the blood of Jesus** over your body — forehead, hands, feet.
4. **Break monitoring spirits, soul ties, and legal rights** tied to marks (see scriptures below).
5. **Remove physical tattoos or items** (as led) that are linked to dark covenants.

Group Application – Rebranding in Christ

- Ask group members: Have you ever had a mark or dream of being branded?

- Lead a prayer of **cleansing and rededication** to Christ.
- Anoint foreheads with oil and declare: *"You now bear the mark of the Lord Jesus Christ."*
- Break off monitoring spirits and rewire their identity in Christ.

Ministry Tools:

- Olive oil (blessed for anointing)
- Mirror or white cloth (symbolic washing act)
- Communion (seal the new identity

Key Insight

What is marked in the spirit is **seen in the spirit** — remove what the enemy used to tag you.

Reflection Journal

- Have I ever seen strange marks, bruises, or symbols on my body without explanation?
- Are there objects, piercings, or tattoos I need to renounce or remove?
- Have I fully rededicated my body as a temple of the Holy Spirit?

Prayer of Rebranding

Lord Jesus, I renounce every mark, covenant, and dedication made in my body or spirit outside of Your will. By Your blood, I erase every satanic brand. I declare that I am marked for Christ alone. Let Your seal of ownership be upon me, and let every monitoring spirit lose track of me now. I am no longer visible to darkness. I walk free — in Jesus' name, Amen.

DAY 15: THE MIRROR REALM — ESCAPING THE PRISON OF REFLECTIONS

"*For now we see through a glass, darkly; but then face to face...*" — 1 Corinthians 13:12

"*They have eyes but cannot see, ears but cannot hear...*" — Psalm 115:5-6

There is a **mirror realm** in the spirit world — a place of *counterfeit identities*, spiritual manipulation, and dark reflections. What many see in dreams or visions may be mirrors not from God, but tools of deception from the dark kingdom.

In the occult, mirrors are used to **trap souls**, **monitor lives**, or **transfer personalities**. In some deliverance sessions, people report seeing themselves "living" in another place — inside a mirror, on a screen, or behind a spiritual veil. These are not hallucinations. They are often satanic prisons designed to:

- Fragment the soul
- Delay destiny
- Confuse identity
- Host alternate spiritual timelines

The goal? To create a *false version* of you that lives under demonic control while your real self lives in confusion or defeat.

Global Expressions

- **Africa** – Mirror witchcraft used by sorcerers to monitor, trap, or attack.
- **Asia** – Shamans use bowls of water or polished stones to "see" and summon spirits.

- **Europe** – Black mirror rituals, necromancy through reflections.
- **Latin America** – Scrying through obsidian mirrors in Aztec traditions.
- **North America** – New age mirror portals, mirror gazing for astral travel.

Testimony — "The Girl in the Mirror"
Maria from the Philippines

Maria had dreams of being trapped in a room full of mirrors. Every time she made progress in life, she'd see a version of herself in the mirror pulling her backward. One night during deliverance, she screamed and described seeing herself "walk out of a mirror" into freedom. Her pastor anointed her eyes and led her in renouncing mirror manipulation. Since then, her mental clarity, business, and family life have transformed.

David from Scotland

David, once deep in new age meditation, practiced "mirror shadow work." Over time, he began hearing voices and seeing himself do things he never intended. After accepting Christ, a deliverance minister broke the mirror soul ties and prayed over his mind. David reported feeling like a "fog lifted" for the first time in years.

Action Plan – Break the Mirror Spell

1. **Renounce** all known or unknown involvement with mirrors used spiritually.
2. **Cover all mirrors in your home** with cloth during prayer or fasting (if led).
3. **Anoint your eyes and forehead** — declare you now see only what God sees.
4. **Use Scripture** to declare your identity in Christ, not in false reflection:
    - *Isaiah 43:1*
    - *2 Corinthians 5:17*
    - *John 8:36*

GROUP APPLICATION – Identity Restoration

- Ask: Have you ever had dreams involving mirrors, doubles, or being watched?
- Lead a prayer of identity recovery — declaring freedom from false versions of self.
- Lay hands on the eyes (symbolically or in prayer) and pray for clarity of sight.
- Use a mirror in group to prophetically declare: *"I am who God says I am. Nothing else."*

Ministry Tools:

- White cloth (covering symbols)
- Olive oil for anointing
- Prophetic mirror declaration guide

Key Insight

The enemy loves to distort how you see yourself — because your identity is your access point to destiny.

Reflection Journal

- Have I believed lies about who I am?
- Have I ever participated in mirror rituals or unknowingly allowed mirror witchcraft?
- What does God say about who I am?

Prayer of Freedom from the Mirror Realm

Father in Heaven, I break every covenant with the mirror realm — every dark reflection, spiritual double, and counterfeit timeline. I renounce all false identities. I declare I am who You say I am. By the blood of Jesus, I step out of the prison of reflections and into the fullness of my purpose. From today, I see with the eyes of the Spirit — in truth and clarity. In Jesus' name, Amen.

DAY 16: BREAKING THE BOND OF WORD CURSES — RECLAIMING YOUR NAME, YOUR FUTURE

"Death and life are in the power of the tongue..." — Proverbs 18:21

"No weapon formed against you shall prosper, and every tongue which rises against you in judgment you shall condemn..." — Isaiah 54:17

Words are not just sounds — they are **spiritual containers**, carrying power to bless or to bind. Many people unknowingly walk under the **weight of curses spoken** over them by parents, teachers, spiritual leaders, ex-lovers, or even their own mouths.

Some have heard these before:

- "You will never amount to anything."
- "You're just like your father — useless."
- "Everything you touch fails."
- "If I can't have you, no one will."
- "You're cursed... watch and see."

Words like these, once spoken in anger, hatred, or fear — especially by someone in authority — can become a spiritual snare. Even self-pronounced curses like *"I wish I was never born"* or *"I'll never get married"* can grant the enemy legal ground.

Global Expressions

- **Africa** – Tribal curses, parental curses over rebellion, market-place curses.
- **Asia** – Karma-based word declarations, ancestral vows spoken over children.

- **Latin America** – Brujeria (witchcraft) curses activated by spoken word.
- **Europe** – Spoken hexes, family "prophecies" that self-fulfill.
- **North America** – Verbal abuse, occult chants, self-hate affirmations.

Whether whispered or shouted, curses spoken with emotion and belief carry weight in the spirit.

Testimony — "When My Mother Spoke Death"
Keisha (Jamaica)
Keisha grew up hearing her mother say: *"You're the reason my life is ruined."* Every birthday, something bad would happen. At 21, she attempted suicide, convinced her life had no value. During a deliverance service, the minister asked: *"Who spoke death over your life?"* She broke down. After renouncing the words and releasing forgiveness, she finally experienced joy. Now, she teaches young girls how to speak life over themselves.

Andrei (Romania)
Andrei's teacher once said: *"You will end up in prison or dead before 25."* That statement haunted him. He fell into crime, and at 24 was arrested. In prison, he encountered Christ and realized the curse he had agreed with. He wrote the teacher a forgiveness letter, tore up every lie spoken over him, and began speaking God's promises. He now leads a prison outreach ministry.

Action Plan – Reverse the Curse

1. Write down negative statements spoken over you — by others or yourself.
2. In prayer, **renounce every word curse** (say it out loud).
3. **Release forgiveness** to the person who spoke it.
4. **Speak God's truth** over yourself to replace the curse with blessing:
    - *Jeremiah 29:11*
    - *Deuteronomy 28:13*
    - *Romans 8:37*
    - *Psalm 139:14*

Group Application – The Power of Words

- Ask: What statements have shaped your identity — good or bad?
- In groups, break curses out loud (with sensitivity), and speak blessings in replacement.
- Use scripture cards — each person reads aloud 3 truths about their identity.
- Encourage members to begin a 7-day *Blessing Decree* over themselves.

Ministry Tools:

- Flash cards with scripture identity
- Olive oil to anoint mouths (sanctifying speech)
- Mirror declarations — speak truth over your reflection daily

Key Insight

If a curse was spoken, it can be broken — and a new word of life can be spoken in its place.

Reflection Journal

- Whose words have shaped my identity?
- Have I cursed myself through fear, anger, or shame?
- What does God say about my future?

Prayer to Break Word Curses

Lord Jesus, I renounce every curse spoken over my life — by family, friends, teachers, lovers, and even myself. I forgive every voice that declared failure, rejection, or death. I break the power of those words now, in Jesus' name. I speak blessing, favor, and destiny over my life. I am who You say I am — loved, chosen, healed, and free. In Jesus' name. Amen.

DAY 17: DELIVERANCE FROM CONTROL & MANIPULATION

"Witchcraft is not always robes and cauldrons — sometimes it's words, emotions, and invisible leashes."

"For rebellion is as the sin of witchcraft, and stubbornness is as iniquity and idolatry."

— 1 Samuel 15:23

Witchcraft isn't only found in shrines. It often wears a smile and manipulates through guilt, threats, flattery, or fear. The Bible equates rebellion — especially the rebellion that exerts ungodly control over others — with witchcraft. Anytime we use emotional, psychological, or spiritual pressure to dominate another's will, we are walking in a dangerous territory.

Global Manifestations

- **Africa** – Mothers cursing children in anger, lovers tying others through "juju" or love potions, spiritual leaders intimidating followers.
- **Asia** – Guru-control over disciples, parental blackmail in arranged marriages, energy cord manipulations.
- **Europe** – Freemason oaths controlling generational behavior, religious guilt and domination.
- **Latin America** – Brujería (witchcraft) used to keep partners, emotional blackmail rooted in family curses.
- **North America** – Narcissistic parenting, manipulative leadership masked as "spiritual covering," fear-based prophecy.

The voice of witchcraft often whispers: *"If you don't do this, you'll lose me, lose God's favor, or suffer."*

But true love never manipulates. God's voice always brings peace, clarity, and freedom of choice.

Real Story — Breaking the Invisible Leash

Grace from Canada was deeply involved in a prophetic ministry where the leader began dictating who she could date, where she could live, and even how to pray. At first, it felt spiritual, but over time, she felt like a prisoner to his opinions. Whenever she tried to make an independent decision, she was told she was "rebelling against God." After a breakdown and reading *Greater Exploits 14*, she realized this was charismatic witchcraft — control masquerading as prophecy.

Grace renounced the soul tie to her spiritual leader, repented for her own agreement with manipulation, and joined a local community for healing. Today, she is whole and helping others come out of religious abuse.

Action Plan — Discerning Witchcraft in Relationships

1. Ask yourself: *Do I feel free around this person, or afraid to disappoint them?*
2. List relationships where guilt, threats, or flattery are used as tools of control.
3. Renounce every emotional, spiritual, or soul tie that makes you feel dominated or voiceless.
4. Pray aloud to break every manipulative leash in your life.

Scripture Tools

- **1 Samuel 15:23** – Rebellion and witchcraft
- **Galatians 5:1** – "Stand firm... do not be burdened again by a yoke of slavery."
- **2 Corinthians 3:17** – "Where the Spirit of the Lord is, there is liberty."
- **Micah 3:5–7** – False prophets using intimidation and bribery

Group Discussion & Application

- Share (anonymously if needed) a time you felt spiritually or

emotionally manipulated.
- Roleplay a "truth-telling" prayer — releasing control over others and taking back your will.
- Have members write letters (real or symbolic) breaking ties with controlling figures and declaring freedom in Christ.

Ministry Tools:

- Pair deliverance partners.
- Use anointing oil to declare freedom over the mind and will.
- Use communion to reestablish covenant with Christ as the *only true covering*.

Key Insight

Where manipulation lives, witchcraft thrives. But where God's Spirit is, there is freedom.

Reflection Journal

- Who or what have I allowed to control my voice, will, or direction?
- Have I ever used fear or flattery to get my way?
- What steps will I take today to walk in the freedom of Christ?

Prayer of Deliverance

Heavenly Father, I renounce every form of emotional, spiritual, and psychological manipulation operating in or around me. I cut off every soul tie rooted in fear, guilt, and control. I break free from rebellion, domination, and intimidation. I declare that I am led by Your Spirit alone. I receive grace to walk in love, truth, and liberty. In Jesus' name. Amen.

DAY 18: BREAKING THE POWER OF UNFORGIVENESS & BITTERNESS

"*Unforgiveness is like drinking poison and expecting the other person to die.*"

"**See to it... that no bitter root grows up to cause trouble and defile many.**"

— *Hebrews 12:15*

Bitterness is a silent destroyer. It may begin with hurt — a betrayal, a lie, a loss — but when left unchecked, it festers into unforgiveness, and finally, into a root that poisons everything.

Unforgiveness opens the door for tormenting spirits (Matthew 18:34). It clouds discernment, hinders healing, chokes your prayers, and blocks the flow of God's power.

Deliverance is not just about casting demons out — it's about releasing what you've been holding inside.

GLOBAL EXPRESSIONS of Bitterness

- **Africa** – Tribal wars, political violence, and family betrayals passed down generations.
- **Asia** – Dishonor between parents and children, caste-based wounds, religious betrayals.
- **Europe** – Generational silence over abuse, bitterness over divorce or infidelity.
- **Latin America** – Wounds from corrupt institutions, family rejections, spiritual manipulation.
- **North America** – Church hurt, racial trauma, absent fathers,

workplace injustice.

Bitterness doesn't always shout. Sometimes, it whispers, "I'll never forget what they did."

But God says: *Let it go — not because they deserve it, but because **you** do.*

Real Story — The Woman Who Wouldn't Forgive

Maria from Brazil was 45 when she first came for deliverance. Every night, she dreamed of being strangled. She had ulcers, high blood pressure, and depression. During the session, it was revealed that she had harbored hatred toward her father who abused her as a child — and later abandoned the family.

She had become a Christian, but had never forgiven him.

As she wept and released him before God, her body convulsed — something broke. That night, she slept peacefully for the first time in 20 years. Two months later, her health began to drastically improve. She now shares her story as a healing coach for women.

Action Plan — Pulling Out the Bitter Root

1. **Name it** – Write down the names of those who hurt you — even yourself or God (if you've been secretly angry with Him).
2. **Release it** – Say out loud: *"I choose to forgive [name] for [specific offense]. I release them and free myself."*
3. **Burn it** – If safe to do so, burn or shred the paper as a prophetic act of release.
4. **Pray blessings** over those who wronged you — even if your emotions resist. This is spiritual warfare.

Scripture Tools

- *Matthew 18:21–35* – The parable of the unforgiving servant
- *Hebrews 12:15* – Bitter roots defile many
- *Mark 11:25* – Forgive, so your prayers are not hindered
- *Romans 12:19–21* – Leave vengeance to God

GROUP APPLICATION & Ministry

- Ask each person (privately or in writing) to name someone they struggle to forgive.
- Break into prayer teams to walk through the forgiveness process using the prayer below.
- Lead a prophetic "burning ceremony" where written offenses are destroyed and replaced with declarations of healing.

Ministry Tools:

- Forgiveness declaration cards
- Soft instrumental music or soaking worship
- Oil of gladness (for anointing after release)

Key Insight

Unforgiveness is a gate the enemy exploits. Forgiveness is a sword that cuts the cord of bondage.

Reflection Journal

- Who do I need to forgive today?
- Have I forgiven myself — or am I punishing myself for past mistakes?
- Do I believe God can restore what I lost through betrayal or offense?

Prayer of Release

Lord Jesus, I come before You with my pain, anger, and memories. I choose today — by faith — to forgive everyone who has hurt, abused, betrayed, or rejected me. I let them go. I release them from judgment and I release myself from bitterness. I ask You to heal every wound and fill me with Your peace. In Jesus' name. Amen.

DAY 19: HEALING FROM SHAME & CONDEMNATION

"*Shame says, 'I am bad.' Condemnation says, 'I'll never be free.' But Jesus says, 'You are Mine, and I have made you new.'*"

"Those who look to Him are radiant; their faces are never covered with shame."

— *Psalm 34:5*

Shame is not just a feeling — it is a strategy of the enemy. It is the cloak he wraps around those who have fallen, failed, or been violated. It says, "You can't come close to God. You're too filthy. Too damaged. Too guilty."

But condemnation is a **lie** — because in Christ, **there is no condemnation** (Romans 8:1).

Many people seeking deliverance remain stuck because they believe they are **unworthy of freedom**. They carry guilt like a badge and replay their worst mistakes like a broken record.

Jesus didn't just pay for your sins — He paid for your shame.

Global Faces of Shame

- **Africa** – Cultural taboos around rape, barrenness, childlessness, or failure to marry.
- **Asia** – Dishonor-based shame from family expectations or religious defection.
- **Latin America** – Guilt from abortions, occult involvement, or family disgrace.
- **Europe** – Hidden shame from secret sins, abuse, or mental health struggles.
- **North America** – Shame from addiction, divorce, pornography, or identity confusion.

Shame thrives in silence — but it dies in the light of God's love.

True Story — A New Name After Abortion

Jasmine from the U.S. had three abortions before coming to Christ. Though she was saved, she couldn't forgive herself. Every Mother's Day felt like a curse. When people talked about children or parenting, she felt invisible — and worse, unworthy.

During a women's retreat, she heard a message on Isaiah 61 — "instead of shame, a double portion." She wept. That night, she wrote letters to her unborn children, repented again before the Lord, and received a vision of Jesus handing her new names: *"Beloved," "Mother," "Restored."*

She now ministers to post-abortive women and helps them reclaim their identities in Christ.

Action Plan — Step Out of the Shadows

1. **Name the Shame** – Journal what you've been hiding or feeling guilty about.
2. **Confess the Lie** – Write out the accusations you've believed (e.g., "I'm dirty," "I'm disqualified").
3. **Replace with Truth** – Declare aloud God's Word over yourself (see Scriptures below).
4. **Prophetic Action** – Write the word "SHAME" on a piece of paper, then tear or burn it. Declare: *"I am no longer bound by this!"*

Scripture Tools

- *Romans 8:1–2* – No condemnation in Christ
- *Isaiah 61:7* – Double portion for shame
- *Psalm 34:5* – Radiance in His presence
- *Hebrews 4:16* – Bold access to God's throne
- *Zephaniah 3:19–20* – God removes shame among the nations

Group Application & Ministry

- Invite participants to write anonymous shame statements (e.g., "I had an abortion," "I was abused," "I committed fraud") and place them in a sealed box.
- Read Isaiah 61 aloud, then lead a prayer for exchange — mourning for joy, ashes for beauty, shame for honor.
- Play worship music that emphasizes identity in Christ.
- Speak prophetic words over individuals who are ready to let go.

Ministry Tools:

- Identity declaration cards
- Anointing oil
- Worship playlist with songs like "You Say" (Lauren Daigle), "No Longer Slaves," or "Who You Say I Am"

Key Insight

Shame is a thief. It steals your voice, your joy, and your authority. Jesus didn't just forgive your sins — He stripped shame of its power.

Reflection Journal

- What is the earliest memory of shame I can recall?
- What lie have I been believing about myself?
- Am I ready to see myself as God sees me — clean, radiant, and chosen?

Prayer of Healing

Lord Jesus, I bring You my shame, my hidden pain, and every voice of condemnation. I repent of agreeing with the enemy's lies about who I am. I choose to believe what You say — that I am forgiven, loved, and made new. I receive Your robe of righteousness and step into freedom. I walk out of shame and into Your glory. In Jesus' name, Amen.

DAY 20: HOUSEHOLD WITCHCRAFT — WHEN DARKNESS LIVES UNDER THE SAME ROOF

"*Not every enemy is outside. Some wear familiar faces.*"
"A man's enemies will be the members of his own household."
— Matthew 10:36

Some of the fiercest spiritual battles are not fought in forests or shrines — but in bedrooms, kitchens, and family altars.

Household witchcraft refers to demonic operations that originate from within one's family — parents, spouses, siblings, house staff, or extended relatives — through envy, occult practice, ancestral altars, or direct spiritual manipulation.

Deliverance becomes complex when the people involved are **those we love or live with.**

Global Examples of Household Witchcraft

- **Africa** – A jealous stepmother sends curses through food; a sibling invokes spirits against a more successful brother.
- **India & Nepal** – Mothers dedicate children to deities at birth; home altars are used to control destinies.
- **Latin America** – Brujeria or Santeria practiced in secret by relatives to manipulate spouses or children.
- **Europe** – Hidden Freemasonry or occult oaths in family lines; psychic or spiritualist traditions passed down.
- **North America** – Wiccan or new age parents "blessing" their children with crystals, energy cleansing, or tarot.

These powers may hide behind family affection, but their goal is control, stagnation, sickness, and spiritual bondage.

True Story — My Father, the Prophet of the Village

A woman from West Africa grew up in a home where her father was a highly respected village prophet. To outsiders, he was a spiritual guide. Behind closed doors, he buried charms in the compound and made sacrifices on behalf of families seeking favor or revenge.

Strange patterns emerged in her life: repeated nightmares, failed relationships, and unexplainable sickness. When she gave her life to Christ, her father turned against her, declaring she would never succeed without his help. Her life spiraled for years.

After months of midnight prayers and fasting, the Holy Spirit led her to renounce every soul tie with her father's occultic mantle. She buried scriptures in her walls, burned old tokens, and anointed her threshold daily. Slowly, breakthroughs began: her health returned, her dreams cleared, and she finally got married. She now helps other women facing household altars.

Action Plan — Confronting the Familiar Spirit

1. **Discern without dishonor** – Ask God to reveal hidden powers without hatred.
2. **Break soulish agreements** – Renounce every spiritual tie made through rituals, altars, or spoken oaths.
3. **Spiritually separate** – Even if living in the same house, you can **disconnect spiritually** through prayer.
4. **Sanctify your space** – Anoint every room, object, and threshold with oil and scripture.

Scripture Tools

- *Micah 7:5–7* – Trust not in a neighbor
- *Psalm 27:10* – "Though my father and mother forsake me..."
- *Luke 14:26* – Loving Christ more than family
- *2 Kings 11:1–3* – Hidden deliverance from a murderous queen mother
- *Isaiah 54:17* – No weapon formed shall prosper

Group Application

- Share experiences where opposition came from within the family.
- Pray for wisdom, boldness, and love in the face of household resistance.
- Lead a renunciation prayer from every soul tie or spoken curse made by relatives.

Ministry Tools:

- Anointing oil
- Forgiveness declarations
- Covenant release prayers
- Psalm 91 prayer covering

Key Insight

The bloodline can be a blessing or a battlefield. You are called to redeem it, not be ruled by it.

Reflection Journal

- Have I ever had spiritual resistance from someone close?
- Is there someone I need to forgive — even if they're still operating in witchcraft?
- Am I willing to be set apart, even if it costs relationships?

Prayer of Separation & Protection

Father, I acknowledge that the greatest opposition can come from those closest to me. I forgive every household member knowingly or unknowingly working against my destiny. I break every soul tie, curse, and covenant made through my family line that does not align with Your Kingdom. By the blood of Jesus, I sanctify my home and declare: as for me and my house, we shall serve the Lord. Amen.

DAY 21: THE JEZEBEL SPIRIT — SEDUCTION, CONTROL, AND RELIGIOUS MANIPULATION

"*But I have this against you: You tolerate that woman Jezebel, who calls herself a prophetess. By her teaching she misleads...*" — Revelation 2:20

"*Her end will come suddenly, without remedy.*" — Proverbs 6:15

Some spirits shout from the outside.

Jezebel whispers from the inside.

She doesn't just tempt — she **usurps, manipulates, and corrupts**, leaving ministries shattered, marriages suffocated, and nations seduced by rebellion.

What Is the Jezebel Spirit?

The Jezebel spirit:

- Mimics prophecy to mislead
- Uses charm and seduction to control
- Hates true authority and silences prophets
- Masks pride behind false humility
- Often attaches to leadership or those close to it

This spirit can operate through **men or women**, and it thrives where unchecked power, ambition, or rejection go unhealed.

Global Manifestations

- **Africa** – False prophetesses who manipulate altars and demand loyalty with fear.
- **Asia** – Religious mystics mixing seduction with visions to dominate spiritual circles.
- **Europe** – Ancient goddess cults revived in New Age practices under

the name of empowerment.
- **Latin America** – Santeria priestesses wielding control over families through "spiritual advice."
- **North America** – Social media influencers promoting "divine femininity" while mocking biblical submission, authority, or purity.

Real Story: *The Jezebel That Sat on the Altar*

In a Caribbean nation, a church on fire for God began to dim — slowly, subtly. The intercessory group that once met for midnight prayers began to scatter. The youth ministry fell into scandal. Marriages in the church started to fail, and the once fiery pastor became indecisive and spiritually weary.

At the center of it all was a woman — **Sister R.** Beautiful, charismatic, and generous, she was admired by many. She always had a "word from the Lord" and a dream about everyone else's destiny. She gave generously to church projects and earned a seat close to the pastor.

Behind the scenes, she subtly **slandered other women**, seduced a junior pastor, and sowed seeds of division. She positioned herself as a spiritual authority while quietly undermining the actual leadership.

One night, a teenage girl in the church had a vivid dream — she saw a snake coiled beneath the pulpit, whispering into the microphone. Terrified, she shared it with her mother who brought it to the pastor.

The leadership decided to go on a **3-day fast** to seek God's guidance. On the third day, during a prayer session, Sister R began to manifest violently. She hissed, screamed, and accused others of witchcraft. A powerful deliverance followed, and she confessed: she had been initiated into a spiritual order in her late teens, tasked with **infiltrating churches to "steal their fire."**

She had already been in **five churches** before this one. Her weapon wasn't loud — it was **flattery, seduction, emotional control**, and prophetic manipulation.

Today, that church has rebuilt its altar. The pulpit has been re-dedicated. And that young teenage girl? She's now a fiery evangelist who leads a women's prayer movement.

Action Plan — How to Confront Jezebel

1. **Repent** of any way you've cooperated with manipulation, sexual

control, or spiritual pride.
2. **Discern** Jezebel's traits — flattery, rebellion, seduction, false prophecy.
3. **Break soul ties** and unholy alliances in prayer — especially with anyone who draws you away from God's voice.
4. **Declare your authority** in Christ. Jezebel fears those who know who they are.

Scripture Arsenal:

- 1 Kings 18–21 – Jezebel vs Elijah
- Revelation 2:18–29 – Christ's warning to Thyatira
- Proverbs 6:16–19 – What God hates
- Galatians 5:19–21 – Works of the flesh

Group Application

- Discuss: Have you ever witnessed spiritual manipulation? How did it disguise itself?
- As a group, declare a "no tolerance" policy for Jezebel — in church, home, or leadership.
- If needed, go through a **deliverance prayer** or fast to break her influence.
- Rededicate any ministry or altar that's been compromised.

Ministry Tools:
Use anointing oil. Create space for confession and forgiveness. Sing worship songs that proclaim the **Lordship of Jesus.**

Key Insight
Jezebel thrives where **discernment is low** and **tolerance is high**. Her reign ends when spiritual authority awakens.

Reflection Journal

- Have I allowed manipulation to lead me?
- Are there people or influences I've elevated above God's voice?

- Have I silenced my prophetic voice out of fear or control?

Prayer of Deliverance

Lord Jesus, I renounce every alliance with the Jezebel spirit. I reject seduction, control, false prophecy, and manipulation. Cleanse my heart of pride, fear, and compromise. I take back my authority. Let every altar Jezebel has built in my life be torn down. I enthrone You, Jesus, as Lord over my relationships, calling, and ministry. Fill me with discernment and boldness. In Your name, Amen.

DAY 22: PYTHONS AND PRAYERS — BREAKING THE SPIRIT OF CONSTRICTION

"*Once when we were going to the place of prayer, we were met by a female slave who had a spirit of Python...*" — Acts 16:16

"*You shall tread upon the lion and the adder...*" — Psalm 91:13

There's a spirit that doesn't bite — it **squeezes**.

It suffocates your fire.

It coils around your prayer life, your breath, your worship, your discipline — until you begin to give up on what once gave you strength.

This is the spirit of **Python** — a demonic force that **constricts spiritual growth, delays destiny, strangles prayer, and counterfeits prophecy**.

Global Manifestations

- **Africa** – The python spirit appears as false prophetic power, operating in marine and forest shrines.
- **Asia** – Snake spirits worshipped as deities that must be fed or appeased.
- **Latin America** – Santeria serpentine altars used for wealth, lust, and power.
- **Europe** – Serpent symbols in witchcraft, fortune-telling, and psychic circles.
- **North America** – Counterfeit "prophetic" voices rooted in rebellion and spiritual confusion.

Testimony: *The Girl Who Couldn't Breathe*

Marisol from Colombia began having shortness of breath every time she knelt to pray. Her chest would tighten. Her dreams were filled with images of snakes, coiling around her neck or resting under her bed. Doctors found nothing medically wrong.

One day, her grandmother admitted Marisol had been "dedicated" as a child to a mountain spirit known to appear as a serpent. It was a **"protector spirit"**, but it came with a cost.

During a deliverance meeting, Marisol began to scream violently as hands were laid on her. She felt something move in her belly, up her chest, and then out of her mouth like air being expelled.

After that encounter, the breathlessness ended. Her dreams changed. She began leading prayer meetings — the very thing the enemy once tried to strangle out of her.

Signs You May Be Under the Influence of the Python Spirit

- Fatigue and heaviness whenever you try to pray or worship
- Prophetic confusion or deceptive dreams
- Constant feelings of being choked, blocked, or bound
- Depression or despair without clear cause
- Loss of spiritual desire or motivation

Action Plan – Breaking Constriction

1. **Repent** of any occult, psychic, or ancestral involvement.
2. **Declare your body and spirit as God's alone.**
3. **Fast and war** using Isaiah 27:1 and Psalm 91:13.
4. **Anoint your throat, chest, and feet** — claiming freedom to speak, breathe, and walk in truth.

Deliverance Scriptures:

- Acts 16:16–18 – Paul casts out the python spirit
- Isaiah 27:1 – God punishes Leviathan, the fleeing serpent
- Psalm 91 – Protection and authority
- Luke 10:19 – Power to trample snakes and scorpions

GROUP APPLICATION

- Ask: What's choking our prayer life — personally and corporately?
- Lead a group breathing prayer — declaring the **breath of God** (Ruach) over every member.
- Break every false prophetic influence or serpent-like pressure in worship and intercession.

Ministry Tools: Worship with flutes or breath instruments, symbolic cutting of ropes, prayer scarves for breathing freedom.

Key Insight

The Python spirit suffocates what God wants to birth. It must be confronted to recover your breath and boldness.

Reflection Journal

- When did I last feel fully free in prayer?
- Are there signs of spiritual fatigue that I've been ignoring?
- Have I unknowingly accepted "spiritual advice" that brought more confusion?

Prayer of Deliverance

Father, in the name of Jesus, I break every constricting spirit assigned to choke my purpose. I renounce the python spirit and all false prophetic voices. I receive the breath of Your Spirit and declare: I shall breathe freely, pray boldly, and walk uprightly. Every serpent coiled around my life is cut off and cast out. I receive deliverance now. Amen.

DAY 23: THRONES OF INIQUITY — TEARING DOWN TERRITORIAL STRONGHOLDS

"*Shall the throne of iniquity, which devises evil by law, have fellowship with You?*" — Psalm 94:20

"*We wrestle not against flesh and blood, but against... rulers of darkness...*" — Ephesians 6:12

There are invisible **thrones** — established in cities, nations, families, and systems — where demonic powers **rule legally** through covenants, legislation, idolatry, and prolonged rebellion.

These are not random attacks. These are **enthroned authorities**, deeply rooted in structures that perpetuate evil across generations.

Until these thrones are **dismantled spiritually**, the cycles of darkness will persist — no matter how much prayer is offered at the surface level.

Global Strongholds and Thrones

- **Africa** – Thrones of witchcraft in royal bloodlines and traditional councils.
- **Europe** – Thrones of secularism, freemasonry, and legalized rebellion.
- **Asia** – Thrones of idolatry in ancestral temples and political dynasties.
- **Latin America** – Thrones of narco-terror, death cults, and corruption.
- **North America** – Thrones of perversion, abortion, and racial oppression.

These thrones influence decisions, suppress truth, and **devour destinies**.

Testimony: *Deliverance of a City Councilor*

In a city in Southern Africa, a newly elected Christian councilor discovered every officeholder before him had either gone mad, divorced, or died suddenly.

After days of prayer, the Lord revealed a **throne of blood sacrifice** buried beneath the municipal building. A local seer had long ago planted charms as part of a territorial claim.

The councilor gathered intercessors, fasted, and held worship at midnight inside the council chambers. Over three nights, staff members reported strange screams in the walls, and the power flickered.

Within a week, confessions began. Corrupt contracts were exposed, and within months, public services improved. The throne had fallen.

Action Plan – Dethroning Darkness

1. **Identify the throne** — ask the Lord to show you territorial strongholds in your city, office, bloodline, or region.
2. **Repent on behalf of the land** (Daniel 9-style intercession).
3. **Worship strategically** — thrones crumble when God's glory takes over (see 2 Chron. 20).
4. **Declare the name of Jesus** as the only true King over that domain.

Anchor Scriptures:

- Psalm 94:20 – Thrones of iniquity
- Ephesians 6:12 – Rulers and authorities
- Isaiah 28:6 – Spirit of justice for those who take up battle
- 2 Kings 23 – Josiah destroys idolatrous altars and thrones

GROUP ENGAGEMENT

- Conduct a "spiritual map" session of your neighborhood or city.
- Ask: What are the cycles of sin, pain, or oppression here?
- Appoint "watchmen" to pray weekly at key gate locations: schools, courts, markets.
- Lead group decrees against spiritual rulers using Psalm 149:5–9.

Ministry Tools: Shofars, city maps, olive oil for ground consecration, prayer walking guides.

Key Insight

If you want to see transformation in your city, **you must challenge the throne behind the system** — not just the face in front of it.

Reflection Journal

- Are there recurring battles in my city or family that feel bigger than me?
- Have I inherited a battle against a throne I didn't enthrone?
- What "rulers" need to be unseated in prayer?

Prayer of War

O Lord, expose every throne of iniquity ruling over my territory. I declare the name of Jesus as the only King! Let every hidden altar, law, pact, or power enforcing darkness be scattered by fire. I take my place as an intercessor. By the blood of the Lamb and the word of my testimony, I tear down thrones and enthrone Christ over my home, city, and nation. In Jesus' name. Amen.

DAY 24: SOUL FRAGMENTS — WHEN PARTS OF YOU ARE MISSING

"*He restores my soul...*" — Psalm 23:3

"*I will heal your wounds, declares the Lord, because you are called an outcast...*" — Jeremiah 30:17

Trauma has a way of shattering the soul. Abuse. Rejection. Betrayal. Sudden fear. Prolonged grief. These experiences don't just leave memories — they **fracture your inner man**.

Many people walk around looking whole but living with **pieces of themselves missing**. Their joy is splintered. Their identity is scattered. They are trapped in emotional time zones — part of them stuck in a painful past, while the body keeps aging forward.

These are **soul fragments** — parts of your emotional, psychological, and spiritual self that are broken off due to trauma, demonic interference, or witchcraft manipulation.

Until those pieces are gathered, healed, and reintegrated through Jesus, **true freedom remains elusive**.

Global Soul Theft Practices

- **Africa** – Witch doctors capturing people's "essence" in jars or mirrors.
- **Asia** – Soul entrapment rituals by gurus or tantric practitioners.
- **Latin America** – Shamanic soul splitting for control or curses.
- **Europe** – Occult mirror magic used to fracture identity or steal favor.
- **North America** – Trauma from molestation, abortion, or identity confusion often creates deep soul wounds and fragmentation.

Story: *The Girl Who Couldn't Feel*

Andrea, a 25-year-old from Spain, had endured years of molestation from a family member. Though she had accepted Jesus, she remained emotionally numb. She couldn't cry, love, or feel empathy.

A visiting minister asked her a strange question: "Where did you leave your joy?" As Andrea closed her eyes, she remembered being 9 years old, curled in a closet, telling herself, "I'll never feel again."

They prayed together. Andrea forgave, renounced inner vows, and invited Jesus into that specific memory. She wept uncontrollably for the first time in years. That day, **her soul was restored**.

Action Plan – Soul Retrieval & Healing

1. Ask the Holy Spirit: *Where did I lose part of myself?*
2. Forgive anyone involved in that moment, and **renounce inner vows** like "I'll never trust again."
3. Invite Jesus into the memory, and speak healing into that moment.
4. Pray: *"Lord, restore my soul. I call every fragment of me to return and be made whole."*

Key Scriptures:

- Psalm 23:3 – He restores the soul
- Luke 4:18 – Healing the brokenhearted
- 1 Thessalonians 5:23 – Spirit, soul, and body preserved
- Jeremiah 30:17 – Healing for outcasts and wounds

Group Application

- Lead members through a guided **inner healing prayer session**.
- Ask: *Are there moments in your life where you stopped trusting, feeling, or dreaming?*
- Roleplay "returning to that room" with Jesus and watching Him heal the wound.
- Have trusted leaders lay hands gently on heads and declare restoration of soul.

Ministry Tools: Worship music, soft lighting, tissues, journaling prompts.

Key Insight

Deliverance is not just casting out demons. It's **gathering the broken pieces and restoring identity**.

Reflection Journal

- What traumatic events still control how I think or feel today?
- Did I ever say, "I'll never love again," or "I can't trust anyone anymore"?
- What does "wholeness" look like to me — and am I ready for it?

PRAYER OF RESTORATION

Jesus, You are the Shepherd of my soul. I bring You every place where I've been shattered — by fear, shame, pain, or betrayal. I break every inner vow and curse spoken in trauma. I forgive those who wounded me. Now, I call every piece of my soul to return. Restore me fully — spirit, soul, and body. I am not broken forever. I am whole in You. In Jesus' name. Amen.

DAY 25: THE CURSE OF STRANGE CHILDREN — WHEN DESTINIES ARE EXCHANGED AT BIRTH

"*Their children are strange children: now shall a month devour them with their portions.*" — Hosea 5:7

"*Before I formed you in the womb I knew you...*" — Jeremiah 1:5

Not every child born into a home was meant for that home.

Not every child carrying your DNA is carrying your legacy.

The enemy has long used **birth as a battleground** — exchanging destinies, planting counterfeit offspring, initiating babies into dark covenants, and tampering with wombs before conception even begins.

This is not just a physical issue. It is **a spiritual transaction** — involving altars, sacrifices, and demonic legalities.

What Are Strange Children?

"Strange children" are:

- Children born through occult dedication, rituals, or sexual covenants.
- Offspring switched at birth (either spiritually or physically).
- Children carrying dark assignments into a family or lineage.
- Souls captured in the womb via witchcraft, necromancy, or generational altars.

Many children grow up in rebellion, addiction, hatred of parents or self — not just from bad parenting but because of **who claimed them spiritually at birth**.

GLOBAL EXPRESSIONS

- **Africa** – Spiritual exchanges in hospitals, womb pollution through marine spirits or ritual sex.
- **India** – Children initiated into temples or karma-based destinies before birth.
- **Haiti & Latin America** – Santeria dedications, children conceived on altars or after spells.
- **Western Nations** – IVF and surrogacy practices sometimes tied to occult contracts or donor lineages; abortions that leave spiritual doors open.
- **Indigenous Cultures Worldwide** – Spirit naming ceremonies or totemic transfers of identity.

Story: *The Baby with the Wrong Spirit*

Clara, a nurse from Uganda, shared how a woman brought her newborn to a prayer meeting. The child screamed constantly, rejected milk, and reacted violently to prayer.

A prophetic word revealed the baby had been "exchanged" in the spirit at birth. The mother confessed a witch doctor had prayed over her belly while she was desperate for a child.

Through repentance and intense deliverance prayers, the baby went limp, then peaceful. The child later thrived — showing signs of restored peace and development.

Not all affliction in children is natural. Some are **assignments from conception**.

Action Plan – Reclaiming Womb Destiny

1. If you're a parent, **dedicate your child afresh to Jesus Christ**.
2. Renounce any prenatal curses, dedications, or covenants — even unknowingly made by ancestors.
3. Speak directly to your child's spirit in prayer: *"You belong to God. Your destiny is restored."*
4. If childless, pray over your womb, rejecting all forms of spiritual manipulation or tampering.

Key Scriptures:

- Hosea 9:11–16 – Judgment on strange seed
- Isaiah 49:25 – Contending for your children
- Luke 1:41 – Spirit-filled children from the womb
- Psalm 139:13–16 – God's intentional design in the womb

Group Engagement

- Have parents bring names or photos of their children.
- Declare over each name: "Your child's identity is restored. Every strange hand is cut off."
- Pray for spiritual womb cleansing for all women (and men as spiritual carriers of seed).
- Use communion to symbolize reclaiming bloodline destiny.

Ministry Tools: Communion, anointing oil, printed names or baby items (optional).

Key Insight

Satan targets the womb because **that's where prophets, warriors, and destinies are formed**. But every child can be reclaimed through Christ.

Reflection Journal

- Have I ever had strange dreams during pregnancy or after birth?
- Are my children struggling in ways that seem unnatural?
- Am I ready to confront the spiritual origins of generational rebellion or delay?

Prayer of Reclamation

Father, I bring my womb, my seed, and my children to Your altar. I repent for any door — known or unknown — that gave the enemy access. I break every curse, dedication, and demonic assignment tied to my children. I speak over them: You are holy, chosen, and sealed for God's glory. Your destiny is redeemed. In Jesus' name. Amen.

DAY 26: HIDDEN ALTARS OF POWER — BREAKING FREE FROM ELITE OCCULTIC COVENANTS

"*Again, the devil took Him to a very high mountain and showed Him all the kingdoms of the world and their glory. 'All this I will give You,' he said, 'if You will bow down and worship me.'*" — Matthew 4:8–9

Many think satanic power is found only in backroom rituals or dark villages. But some of the most dangerous covenants are hidden behind polished suits, elite clubs, and multi-generational influence.

These are **altars of power** — formed by blood oaths, initiations, secret symbols, and spoken pledges that bind individuals, families, and even entire nations to Lucifer's dominion. From Freemasonry to Kabbalistic rites, from Eastern star initiations to ancient Egyptian and Babylonian mystery schools — they promise enlightenment but deliver bondage.

Global Connections

- **Europe & North America** – Freemasonry, Rosicrucianism, Order of the Golden Dawn, Skull & Bones, Bohemian Grove, Kabbalah initiations.
- **Africa** – Political blood pacts, ancestral spirit bargains for rulership, high-level witchcraft alliances.
- **Asia** – Illuminated societies, dragon spirit pacts, bloodline dynasties tied to ancient sorcery.
- **Latin America** – Political Santeria, cartel-linked ritual protection, pacts made for success and immunity.
- **Middle East** – Ancient Babylonian, Assyrian rites passed down under religious or royal guise.

Testimony – A Freemason's Grandson Finds Freedom

Carlos, raised in an influential family in Argentina, never knew that his grandfather had reached the 33rd degree of Freemasonry. Strange manifestations had plagued his life — sleep paralysis, relational sabotage, and a consistent inability to make progress, no matter how hard he tried.

After attending a deliverance teaching that exposed elite occult links, he confronted his family history and found masonic regalia and hidden journals. During a midnight fast, he renounced every blood covenant and declared freedom in Christ. That very week, he received the job breakthrough he had waited on for years.

High-level altars create high-level opposition — but the **blood of Jesus** speaks louder than any oath or ritual.

Action Plan – Exposing the Hidden Lodge

1. **Investigate**: Are there masonic, esoteric, or secret affiliations in your bloodline?
2. **Renounce** every known and unknown covenant using declarations based on Matthew 10:26–28.
3. **Burn or remove** any occult symbols: pyramids, all-seeing eyes, compasses, obelisks, rings, or robes.
4. **Pray aloud**:

"I break every hidden agreement with secret societies, light cults, and false brotherhoods. I serve only the Lord Jesus Christ."

Group Application

- Have members write out any known or suspected elite occult ties.
- Lead a **symbolic act of cutting ties** — tearing papers, burning images, or anointing their foreheads as a seal of separation.
- Use **Psalm 2** to declare the breaking of national and family conspiracies against the Lord's anointed.

Key Insight

Satan's greatest grip is often clothed in secrecy and prestige. True freedom begins when you expose, renounce, and displace those altars with worship and truth.

Reflection Journal

- Have I inherited wealth, power, or opportunities that feel spiritually "off"?
- Are there secret connections in my ancestry that I've ignored?
- What will it cost me to sever ungodly access to power — and am I willing?

Prayer of Deliverance

Father, I come out of every hidden lodge, altar, and agreement — in my name or on behalf of my bloodline. I sever every soul tie, every blood tie, and every oath made knowingly or unknowingly. Jesus, You are my only Light, my only Truth, and my only covering. Let Your fire consume every ungodly link to power, influence, or deception. I receive total freedom, in Jesus' name. Amen.

DAY 27: UNHOLY ALLIANCES — FREEMASONRY, ILLUMINATI & SPIRITUAL INFILTRATION

"*Have nothing to do with the fruitless deeds of darkness, but rather expose them.*" — Ephesians 5:11

"*You cannot drink the cup of the Lord and the cup of demons too.*" — 1 Corinthians 10:21

There are secret societies and global networks that present themselves as harmless fraternal organizations — offering charity, connection, or enlightenment. But behind the curtain lie deeper oaths, blood rituals, soul ties, and layers of Luciferian doctrine cloaked in "light."

Freemasonry, the Illuminati, Eastern Star, Skull and Bones, and their sister networks are not just social clubs. They are altars of allegiance — some dating back centuries — designed to spiritually infiltrate families, governments, and even churches.

Global Footprint

- **North America & Europe** – Freemasonry temples, Scottish Rite lodges, Yale's Skull & Bones.
- **Africa** – Political and royal initiations with masonic rites, blood pacts for protection or power.
- **Asia** – Kabbalah schools masked as mystic enlightenment, secret monastic rites.
- **Latin America** – Hidden elite orders, Santeria merged with elite influence and blood pacts.
- **Middle East** – Ancient Babylonian secret societies tied to power structures and false light worship.

THESE NETWORKS OFTEN:

- Require blood or spoken oaths.
- Use occult symbols (compasses, pyramids, eyes).
- Conduct ceremonies to invoke or dedicate one's soul to an order.
- Grant influence or wealth in exchange for spiritual control.

Testimony – A Bishop's Confession

A bishop in East Africa confessed before his church that he had once joined Freemasonry at a low level during university — simply for "connections." But as he rose through the ranks, he began to see strange requirements: an oath of silence, ceremonies with blindfolds and symbols, and a "light" that made his prayer life cold. He stopped dreaming. He couldn't read Scripture.

After repenting and publicly denouncing every rank and vow, the spiritual fog lifted. Today, he preaches Christ boldly, exposing what he once participated in. The chains were invisible — until broken.

Action Plan – Breaking Freemasonry & Secret Society Influence

1. **Identify** any personal or family involvement with Freemasonry, Rosicrucianism, Kabbalah, Skull and Bones, or similar secret orders.
2. **Renounce each level or degree of initiation**, from 1st to 33rd or higher, including all rituals, tokens, and oaths. (You may find guided deliverance renunciations online.)
3. **Pray with authority**:

"I break every soul tie, blood covenant, and oath made to secret societies — by me or on my behalf. I reclaim my soul for Jesus Christ!"

1. **Destroy symbolic items**: regalia, books, certificates, rings, or framed images.
2. **Declare** freedom using:
    - *Galatians 5:1*
    - *Psalm 2:1–6*
    - *Isaiah 28:15–18*

Group Application

- Have the group close their eyes and ask the Holy Spirit to reveal any secret affiliations or family ties.
- Corporate renunciation: go through a prayer to denounce every known or unknown tie to elite orders.
- Use communion to seal the break and re-align covenants to Christ.
- Anoint heads and hands — restoring clarity of mind and holy works.

Key Insight

What the world calls "elite," God may call an abomination. Not all influence is holy — and not all light is Light. There is no such thing as harmless secrecy when it involves spiritual oaths.

Reflection Journal

- Have I been part of, or curious about, secret orders or mystical enlightenment groups?
- Is there evidence of spiritual blindness, stagnation, or coldness in my faith?
- Do I need to confront family involvement with courage and grace?

Prayer of Freedom

Lord Jesus, I come before You as the only true Light. I renounce every tie, every oath, every false light, and every hidden order that claims me. I cut off Freemasonry, secret societies, ancient brotherhoods, and every spiritual tie linked to darkness. I declare that I am under the blood of Jesus alone — sealed, delivered, and free. Let Your Spirit burn away all residue of these covenants. In Jesus' name, amen.

DAY 28: KABBALAH, ENERGY GRIDS & THE LURE OF MYSTICAL "LIGHT"

"*For Satan himself masquerades as an angel of light.*" — 2 Corinthians 11:14

"*The light in you is darkness—how deep is that darkness!*" — Luke 11:35

In an age obsessed with spiritual enlightenment, many are unknowingly diving into ancient Kabbalistic practices, energy healing, and mystical light teachings rooted in occult doctrines. These teachings often masquerade as "Christian mysticism," "Jewish wisdom," or "science-based spirituality" — but they originate from Babylon, not Zion.

Kabbalah isn't just a Jewish philosophical system; it's a spiritual matrix built on secret codes, divine emanations (Sefirot), and esoteric pathways. It's the same seductive deception behind tarot, numerology, zodiac portals, and New Age grids.

Many celebrities, influencers, and business moguls wear red strings, meditate with crystal energy, or follow the Zohar without knowing they're partaking in an invisible system of spiritual entrapment.

Global Entanglements

- **North America** – Kabbalah centers disguised as wellness spaces; guided energy meditations.
- **Europe** – Druidic Kabbalah and esoteric Christianity taught in secret orders.
- **Africa** – Prosperity cults mixing scripture with numerology and energy portals.
- **Asia** – Chakra healing rebranded as "light activation" aligned with universal codes.
- **Latin America** – Saints mixed with Kabbalistic archangels in mystic

Catholicism.

This is the seduction of false light — where knowledge becomes a god and illumination becomes a prison.

Real Testimony – Escaping the "Light Trap"

Marisol, a South American business coach, thought she had discovered true wisdom through numerology and "divine energy flow" from a Kabbalistic mentor. Her dreams became vivid, her visions sharp. But her peace? Gone. Her relationships? Collapsing.

She found herself tormented by shadowy beings in her sleep, despite her daily "light prayers." A friend sent her a video testimony of a former mystic who encountered Jesus. That night, Marisol called out to Jesus. She saw a blinding white light — not mystical, but pure. Peace returned. She destroyed her materials and began her deliverance journey. Today, she runs a Christ-centered mentoring platform for women trapped in spiritual deception.

Action Plan – Renouncing False Illumination

1. **Audit** your exposure: Have you read mystic books, practiced energy healing, followed horoscopes, or worn red strings?
2. **Repent** for seeking light outside of Christ.
3. **Break ties** with:
   - Kabbalah/Zohar teachings
   - Energy medicine or light activation
   - Angel invocations or name decoding
   - Sacred geometry, numerology, or "codes"
4. **Pray aloud**:

"Jesus, You are the Light of the world. I renounce every false light, every occult teaching, and every mystical trap. I return to You as my only source of truth!"

1. **Scriptures to Declare**:
   - John 8:12
   - Deuteronomy 18:10–12
   - Isaiah 2:6
   - 2 Corinthians 11:13–15

Group Application

- Ask: Have you (or family) ever participated in or been exposed to New Age, numerology, Kabbalah, or mystical "light" teachings?
- Group renunciation of false light and re-dedication to Jesus as the only Light.
- Use salt and light imagery — give each participant a pinch of salt and a candle to declare, "I am salt and light in Christ alone."

Key Insight

Not all light is holy. What illuminates outside of Christ will eventually consume.

Reflection Journal

- Have I sought knowledge, power, or healing outside of the Word of God?
- What spiritual tools or teachings do I need to get rid of?
- Is there anyone I've introduced to New Age or "light" practices I now need to guide back?

Prayer of Deliverance

Father, I come out of agreement with every spirit of false light, mysticism, and secret knowledge. I renounce Kabbalah, numerology, sacred geometry, and every dark code posing as light. I declare Jesus is the Light of my life. I walk away from the path of deception and step into the truth. Purge me with Your fire and fill me with the Holy Spirit. In Jesus' name. Amen.

DAY 29: THE ILLUMINATI VEIL — UNMASKING THE ELITE OCCULT NETWORKS

"The kings of the earth take their stand and the rulers gather together against the Lord and against His Anointed One." — Psalm 2:2

"Nothing is hidden that will not be revealed, and nothing concealed that will not be brought to light." — Luke 8:17

There is a world within our world. Hidden in plain sight.

From Hollywood to high finance, from political corridors to music empires, a network of dark alliances and spiritual contracts governs systems that shape culture, thought, and power. It's more than conspiracy — it's ancient rebellion repackaged for the modern stage.

The Illuminati, at its core, is not simply a secret society — it's a Luciferian agenda. A spiritual pyramid where those at the top pledge allegiance through blood, ritual, and soul exchange, often wrapped in symbols, fashion, and pop culture to condition the masses.

This is not about paranoia. It's about awareness.

REAL STORY – A JOURNEY from Fame to Faith

Marcus was a rising music producer in the U.S. When his third major hit crossed charts, he was introduced to an exclusive club — powerful men and women, spiritual "mentors," contracts soaked in secrecy. At first, it seemed like elite mentorship. Then came the "invocation" sessions — dark rooms, red lights, chants, and mirror rituals. He began to experience out-of-body travels, voices whispering songs to him at night.

One night, under influence and torment, he tried to take his life. But Jesus intervened. A praying grandmother's intercession broke through. He fled, renounced the system, and began a long deliverance journey. Today, he exposes the industry's darkness through music that testifies to the light.

HIDDEN SYSTEMS OF CONTROL

- **Blood Sacrifices & Sex Rituals** – Initiation into power requires exchange: body, blood, or innocence.
- **Mind Programming (MK Ultra patterns)** – Used in media, music, politics to create fractured identities and handlers.
- **Symbolism** – Pyramid eyes, phoenixes, checkerboard floors, owls, and inverted stars – gateways of allegiance.
- **Luciferian Doctrine** – "Do what thou wilt," "Become your own god," "Lightbearer enlightenment."

Action Plan – Breaking Free from Elite Webs

1. **Repent** for participating in any system tied to occult empowerment, even unknowingly (music, media, contracts).
2. **Renounce** fame at all cost, hidden covenants, or fascination with elite lifestyles.
3. **Pray over** every contract, brand, or network you're part of. Ask the Holy Spirit to expose hidden ties.
4. **Declare out loud**:

"I reject every system, oath, and symbol of darkness. I belong to the Kingdom of Light. My soul is not for sale!"

1. **Anchor Scriptures**:
    - Isaiah 28:15–18 – Covenant with death shall not stand
    - Psalm 2 – God laughs at wicked conspiracies
    - 1 Corinthians 2:6–8 – The rulers of this age do not understand God's wisdom

GROUP APPLICATION

- Lead the group in a **symbol cleansing** session — bring images or logos participants have questions about.
- Encourage people to share where they've seen Illuminati signs in pop culture, and how it shaped their views.
- Invite participants to **recommit their influence** (music, fashion, media) to Christ's purpose.

Key Insight

The most powerful deception is the one that hides in glamor. But when the mask is removed, the chains break.

Reflection Journal

- Am I drawn to symbols or movements I don't fully understand?
- Have I made vows or agreements in pursuit of influence or fame?
- What part of my gifting or platform do I need to surrender again to God?

Prayer of Freedom

Father, I reject every hidden structure, oath, and influence of the Illuminati and elite occult. I renounce fame without You, power without purpose, and knowledge without the Holy Spirit. I cancel every blood or word covenant ever made over me, knowingly or unknowingly. Jesus, I enthrone You as Lord over my mind, gifts, and destiny. Expose and destroy every invisible chain. In Your name I rise, and I walk in light. Amen.

DAY 30: THE MYSTERY SCHOOLS — ANCIENT SECRETS, MODERN BONDAGE

"*Their throats are open graves; their tongues practice deceit. The poison of vipers is on their lips.*" — Romans 3:13

"*Do not call conspiracy everything this people calls a conspiracy; do not fear what they fear... The Lord Almighty is the One you are to regard as holy...*" — Isaiah 8:12–13

Long before the Illuminati, there were the ancient mystery schools — Egypt, Babylon, Greece, Persia — designed not only to pass on "knowledge," but to awaken supernatural power through dark rituals. Today, these schools are resurrected in elite universities, spiritual retreats, "awareness" camps, even through online training courses masked as personal development or high-order consciousness awakening.

From Kabbalah circles to Theosophy, Hermetic Orders, and Rosicrucianism — the aim is the same: "to become like gods," awakening latent power without the surrender to God. Hidden chants, sacred geometry, astral projection, pineal gland unlocking, and ceremonial rituals bring many into spiritual bondage under the guise of "light."

But every "light" not rooted in Jesus is a false light. And every hidden oath must be broken.

Real Story – From Adept to Abandoned

Sandra*, a South African wellness coach, was initiated into an Egyptian mystery order through a mentorship program. The training included chakra alignments, sun meditations, moon rituals, and ancient wisdom scrolls. She began to experience "downloads" and "ascensions," but soon these turned into panic attacks, sleep paralysis, and suicidal episodes.

When a deliverance minister exposed the source, Sandra realized her soul was tethered through vows and spiritual contracts. Renouncing the order meant losing income and connections — but she gained her freedom. Today, she runs a healing center centered in Christ, warning others of New Age deception.

Common Threads of Mystery Schools Today

- **Kabbalah Circles** – Jewish mysticism mixed with numerology, angel worship, and astral planes.
- **Hermeticism** – "As above, so below" doctrine; empowering the soul to manipulate reality.
- **Rosicrucians** – Secret orders tied to alchemical transformation and spirit ascension.
- **Freemasonry & Esoteric Fraternities** – Layered progression into hidden light; each degree bound by oaths and rituals.
- **Spiritual Retreats** – Psychedelic "enlightenment" ceremonies with shamans or "guides."

Action Plan – Breaking Ancient Yokes

1. **Renounce** all covenants made through initiations, courses, or spiritual contracts outside Christ.
2. **Cancel** the power of every "light" or "energy" source not rooted in the Holy Spirit.
3. **Cleanse** your home of symbols: ankhs, eye of Horus, sacred geometry, altars, incense, statues, or ritual books.
4. **Declare aloud:**

"I reject every ancient and modern path to false light. I submit to Jesus Christ, the true Light. Every secret oath is broken by His blood."

ANCHOR SCRIPTURES

- Colossians 2:8 – No hollow and deceptive philosophy

- John 1:4–5 – The true Light shines in the darkness
- 1 Corinthians 1:19–20 – God destroys the wisdom of the wise

GROUP APPLICATION

- Host a symbolic "burning of scrolls" night (Acts 19:19) — where group members bring and destroy any occult books, jewelry, items.
- Pray over people who have "downloaded" strange knowledge or opened third-eye chakras through meditation.
- Walk participants through a **"light transfer"** prayer — asking the Holy Spirit to take over every area previously surrendered to occult light.

KEY INSIGHT

God doesn't hide truth in riddles and rituals — He reveals it through His Son. Beware of "light" that draws you into darkness.

REFLECTION JOURNAL

- Have I joined any online or physical school promising ancient wisdom, activation, or mystery powers?
- Are there books, symbols, or rituals I once thought were harmless but now feel convicted about?
- Where have I sought spiritual experience more than relationship with God?

Prayer of Deliverance

Lord Jesus, You are the Way, the Truth, and the Light. I repent for every path I took that bypassed Your Word. I renounce all mystery schools, secret orders, oaths, and initiations. I break soul ties with all guides, teachers, spirits, and systems rooted in ancient deception. Shine Your light in every hidden place of my heart and fill me with the truth of Your Spirit. In Jesus' name, I walk free. Amen.

DAY 31: KABBALAH, SACRED GEOMETRY & ELITE LIGHT DECEPTION

"*For Satan himself transforms himself into an angel of light.*" — 2 Corinthians 11:14

"*The secret things belong to the Lord our God, but the things revealed belong to us...*" — Deuteronomy 29:29

In our quest for spiritual knowledge, there lies a danger — the lure of "hidden wisdom" that promises power, light, and divinity apart from Christ. From celebrity circles to secret lodges, from art to architecture, a pattern of deception weaves its way across the globe, drawing seekers into the esoteric web of **Kabbalah**, **sacred geometry**, and **mystery teachings**.

These are not harmless intellectual explorations. They are entryways into spiritual covenants with fallen angels masquerading as light.

GLOBAL MANIFESTATIONS

- **Hollywood & Music Industry** – Many celebrities openly wear Kabbalah bracelets or tattoo sacred symbols (like the Tree of Life) that trace back to occultic Jewish mysticism.
- **Fashion & Architecture** – Masonic designs and sacred geometrical patterns (the Flower of Life, hexagrams, the Eye of Horus) are embedded into clothing, buildings, and digital art.
- **Middle East & Europe** – Kabbalah study centers thrive among elites, often mixing mysticism with numerology, astrology, and angelic invocations.

- **Online & New Age Circles Worldwide** – YouTube, TikTok, and podcasts normalize "light codes," "energy portals," "3–6–9 vibrations," and "divine matrix" teachings based in sacred geometry and Kabbalistic frameworks.

Real Story — When Light Becomes a Lie

Jana, a 27-year-old from Sweden, began exploring Kabbalah after following her favorite singer who credited it for her "creative awakening." She bought the red string bracelet, began meditating with geometric mandalas, and studied angel names from ancient Hebrew texts.

Things began to shift. Her dreams turned strange. She'd feel beings beside her in her sleep, whispering wisdom — and then demanding blood. Shadows followed her, yet she craved more light.

Eventually, she stumbled upon a deliverance video online and realized her torment was not spiritual ascension, but spiritual deception. After six months of deliverance sessions, fasting, and burning every Kabbalistic object in her house, peace began to return. She now warns others through her blog: "The false light almost destroyed me."

DISCERNING THE PATH

Kabbalah, while sometimes dressed in religious robes, rejects Jesus Christ as the only way to God. It often elevates the **"divine self"**, promotes **channeling** and **tree-of-life ascension**, and uses **mathematical mysticism** to summon power. These practices open **spiritual gates** — not to heaven, but to entities masquerading as light-bearers.

Many Kabbalistic doctrines intersect with:

- Freemasonry
- Rosicrucianism
- Gnosticism
- Luciferian enlightenment cults

The common denominator? The pursuit of godhood without Christ.

Action Plan – Exposing & Evicting False Light

1. **Repent** of every engagement with Kabbalah, numerology, sacred geometry, or "mystery school" teachings.
2. **Destroy objects** in your home linked to these practices — mandalas, altars, Kabbalah texts, crystal grids, sacred symbol jewelry.
3. **Renounce spirits of false light** (e.g., Metatron, Raziel, Shekinah in mystical form) and command every counterfeit angel to leave.
4. **Immerse yourself** in the simplicity and sufficiency of Christ (2 Corinthians 11:3).
5. **Fast & anoint** yourself — eyes, forehead, hands — renouncing all false wisdom and declaring your allegiance to God alone.

Group Application

- Share any encounters with "light teachings," numerology, Kabbalah media, or sacred symbols.
- As a group, list phrases or beliefs that sound "spiritual" but oppose Christ (e.g., "I am divine," "the universe provides," "Christ consciousness").
- Anoint each person with oil while declaring John 8:12 — *"Jesus is the Light of the World."*
- Burn or discard any materials or objects that reference sacred geometry, mysticism, or "divine codes."

KEY INSIGHT

Satan doesn't come first as the destroyer. He often comes as the illuminator — offering secret knowledge and false light. But that light leads only to deeper darkness.

Reflection Journal

- Have I opened my spirit to any "spiritual light" that bypassed Christ?
- Are there symbols, phrases, or objects I thought were harmless but now recognize as portals?
- Have I elevated personal wisdom over biblical truth?

Prayer of Deliverance

Father, I renounce every false light, mystical teaching, and secret knowledge that has entangled my soul. I confess that only Jesus Christ is the true Light of the world. I reject Kabbalah, sacred geometry, numerology, and all doctrines of demons. Let every counterfeit spirit now be uprooted from my life. Cleanse my eyes, my thoughts, my imagination, and my spirit. I am Yours alone — spirit, soul, and body. In Jesus' name. Amen.

DAY 32: THE SERPENT SPIRIT WITHIN — WHEN DELIVERANCE COMES TOO LATE

"*They have eyes full of adultery... they entice unstable souls... they have followed the way of Balaam... for whom is reserved the blackness of darkness forever.*" — 2 Peter 2:14–17

"*Do not be deceived: God cannot be mocked. A man reaps what he sows.*" — Galatians 6:7

There is a demonic counterfeit that parades as enlightenment. It heals, energizes, empowers — but only for a season. It whispers divine mysteries, opens your "third eye," unleashes power in the spine — and then **enslaves you in torment**.

It is **Kundalini**.

The **serpent spirit**.

The false "holy spirit" of the New Age.

Once activated — through yoga, meditation, psychedelics, trauma, or occult rituals — this force coils at the base of the spine and rises like fire through the chakras. Many believe it to be spiritual awakening. In truth, it is **demonic possession** disguised as divine energy.

But what happens when it **won't go away**?

Real Story – "I Can't Turn It Off"

Marissa, a young Christian woman in Canada, had dabbled in "Christian yoga" before giving her life to Christ. She loved the peaceful feelings, the vibrations, the light visions. But after one intense session where she felt her spine "ignite," she blacked out — and woke up unable to breathe. That night, something began **tormenting her sleep**, twisting her body, appearing as "Jesus" in her dreams — but mocking her.

She received **deliverance** five times. The spirits would leave — but return. Her spine still vibrated. Her eyes saw into the spirit realm constantly. Her body would move involuntarily. Despite salvation, she was now walking through a hell few Christians understood. Her spirit was saved — but her soul was **violated, cracked open, and fragmented.**

The Aftermath No One Talks About

- **Third eyes remain open**: Constant visions, hallucinations, spiritual noise, "angels" speaking lies.
- **Body doesn't stop vibrating**: Uncontrollable energy, pressure in the skull, heart palpitations.
- **Unrelenting torment**: Even after 10+ deliverance sessions.
- **Isolation**: Pastors don't understand. Churches ignore the problem. The person is labeled "unstable."
- **Fear of hell**: Not because of sin, but because of the torment that refuses to end.

Can Christians reach a point of no return?

Yes — in this life.

You can be **saved**, but so fragmented that **your soul is in torment until death.**

This is not fear-mongering. This is a **prophetic warning.**

Global Examples

- **Africa** – False prophets releasing Kundalini fire during services — people convulse, foam, laugh, or roar.
- **Asia** – Yoga masters ascending into "siddhi" (demonic possession) and calling it god-consciousness.
- **Europe/North America** – Neo-charismatic movements channeling "glory realms," barking, laughing, falling uncontrollably — not of God.
- **Latin America** – Shamanic awakenings using ayahuasca (plant drugs) to open spiritual doors they can't shut.

ACTION PLAN — IF YOU'VE Gone Too Far

1. **Confess the exact portal**: Kundalini yoga, third-eye meditations, new age churches, psychedelics, etc.
2. **Stop all deliverance chasing**: Some spirits torment longer when you keep empowering them with fear.
3. **Anchor yourself in Scripture** DAILY — especially Psalm 119, Isaiah 61, and John 1. These renew the soul.
4. **Submit to community**: Find at least one Holy Spirit-filled believer to walk with. Isolation empowers demons.
5. **Renounce all spiritual "sight," fire, knowledge, energy** — even if it feels holy.
6. **Ask God for mercy** — Not once. Daily. Hourly. Persist. God may not remove it instantly, but He will carry you.

GROUP APPLICATION

- Hold a time of silent reflection. Ask: Have I pursued spiritual power over spiritual purity?
- Pray over those who have unrelenting torment. Do NOT promise instant freedom — promise **discipleship**.
- Teach the difference between the **fruit of the Spirit** (Galatians 5:22–23) and **soulish manifestations** (shaking, heat, visions).
- Burn or destroy every new age object: chakra symbols, crystals, yoga mats, books, oils, "Jesus cards."

Key Insight

There is a **line** that can be crossed — when the soul becomes an open gateway and refuses to shut. Your spirit may be saved... but your soul and body may still live in torment if you've been defiled by occult light.

Reflection Journal

- Did I ever pursue power, fire, or prophetic sight more than holiness and truth?
- Have I opened doors through "Christianized" new age practices?
- Am I willing to **walk daily** with God even if full deliverance takes years?

Prayer of Survival

Father, I cry out for mercy. I renounce every serpent spirit, Kundalini power, third eye opening, false fire, or new age counterfeit I've ever touched. I surrender my soul — fractured as it is — back to You. Jesus, rescue me not just from sin, but from torment. Seal my gates. Heal my mind. Shut my eyes. Crush the serpent in my spine. I wait for You, even in the pain. And I will not give up. In Jesus' name. Amen.

DAY 33: THE SERPENT SPIRIT WITHIN — WHEN DELIVERANCE COMES TOO LATE

"*They have eyes full of adultery... they entice unstable souls... they have followed the way of Balaam... for whom is reserved the blackness of darkness forever.*" — 2 Peter 2:14–17

"*Do not be deceived: God cannot be mocked. A man reaps what he sows.*" — Galatians 6:7

There is a demonic counterfeit that parades as enlightenment. It heals, energizes, empowers — but only for a season. It whispers divine mysteries, opens your "third eye," unleashes power in the spine — and then **enslaves you in torment**.

It is **Kundalini**.

The **serpent spirit**.

The false "holy spirit" of the New Age.

Once activated — through yoga, meditation, psychedelics, trauma, or occult rituals — this force coils at the base of the spine and rises like fire through the chakras. Many believe it to be spiritual awakening. In truth, it is **demonic possession** disguised as divine energy.

But what happens when it **won't go away?**

Real Story – "I Can't Turn It Off"

Marissa, a young Christian woman in Canada, had dabbled in "Christian yoga" before giving her life to Christ. She loved the peaceful feelings, the vibrations, the light visions. But after one intense session where she felt her spine "ignite," she blacked out — and woke up unable to breathe. That night, something began **tormenting her sleep**, twisting her body, appearing as "Jesus" in her dreams — but mocking her.

She received **deliverance** five times. The spirits would leave — but return. Her spine still vibrated. Her eyes saw into the spirit realm constantly. Her body would move involuntarily. Despite salvation, she was now walking through a hell few Christians understood. Her spirit was saved — but her soul was **violated, cracked open, and fragmented**.

The Aftermath No One Talks About

- **Third eyes remain open**: Constant visions, hallucinations, spiritual noise, "angels" speaking lies.
- **Body doesn't stop vibrating**: Uncontrollable energy, pressure in the skull, heart palpitations.
- **Unrelenting torment**: Even after 10+ deliverance sessions.
- **Isolation**: Pastors don't understand. Churches ignore the problem. The person is labeled "unstable."
- **Fear of hell**: Not because of sin, but because of the torment that refuses to end.

Can Christians reach a point of no return?

Yes — in this life.

You can be **saved**, but so fragmented that **your soul is in torment until death**.

This is not fear-mongering. This is a **prophetic warning**.

Global Examples

- **Africa** – False prophets releasing Kundalini fire during services — people convulse, foam, laugh, or roar.
- **Asia** – Yoga masters ascending into "siddhi" (demonic possession) and calling it god-consciousness.
- **Europe/North America** – Neo-charismatic movements channeling "glory realms," barking, laughing, falling uncontrollably — not of God.
- **Latin America** – Shamanic awakenings using ayahuasca (plant drugs) to open spiritual doors they can't shut.

Action Plan — If You've Gone Too Far

1. **Confess the exact portal**: Kundalini yoga, third-eye meditations, new age churches, psychedelics, etc.
2. **Stop all deliverance chasing**: Some spirits torment longer when you keep empowering them with fear.
3. **Anchor yourself in Scripture** DAILY — especially Psalm 119, Isaiah 61, and John 1. These renew the soul.
4. **Submit to community**: Find at least one Holy Spirit-filled believer to walk with. Isolation empowers demons.
5. **Renounce all spiritual "sight," fire, knowledge, energy** — even if it feels holy.
6. **Ask God for mercy** — Not once. Daily. Hourly. Persist. God may not remove it instantly, but He will carry you.

Group Application

- Hold a time of silent reflection. Ask: Have I pursued spiritual power over spiritual purity?
- Pray over those who have unrelenting torment. Do NOT promise instant freedom — promise **discipleship**.
- Teach the difference between the **fruit of the Spirit** (Galatians 5:22–23) and **soulish manifestations** (shaking, heat, visions).
- Burn or destroy every new age object: chakra symbols, crystals, yoga mats, books, oils, "Jesus cards."

Key Insight

There is a **line** that can be crossed — when the soul becomes an open gateway and refuses to shut. Your spirit may be saved... but your soul and body may still live in torment if you've been defiled by occult light.

Reflection Journal

- Did I ever pursue power, fire, or prophetic sight more than holiness and truth?
- Have I opened doors through "Christianized" new age practices?
- Am I willing to **walk daily** with God even if full deliverance takes years?

Prayer of Survival

Father, I cry out for mercy. I renounce every serpent spirit, Kundalini power, third eye opening, false fire, or new age counterfeit I've ever touched. I surrender my soul — fractured as it is — back to You. Jesus, rescue me not just from sin, but from torment. Seal my gates. Heal my mind. Shut my eyes. Crush the serpent in my spine. I wait for You, even in the pain. And I will not give up. In Jesus' name. Amen.

DAY 34: MASONS, CODES & CURSES — When Brotherhood Becomes Bondage

"*Have no fellowship with the unfruitful works of darkness, but rather expose them.*" — Ephesians 5:11

"*You shall not make a covenant with them or with their gods.*" — Exodus 23:32

Secret societies promise success, connection, and ancient wisdom. They offer **oaths, degrees, and secrets** passed down "for good men." But what most don't realize is: these societies are **covenant altars**, often built on blood, deception, and demonic allegiance.

From Freemasonry to the Kabbalah, Rosicrucians to Skull & Bones — these organizations aren't just clubs. They are **spiritual contracts**, forged in darkness and sealed with rites that **curse generations**.

Some joined willingly. Others had ancestors who did.

Either way, the curse remains — until it is broken.

A Hidden Legacy — Jason's Story

Jason, a successful banker in the U.S., had everything going for him — a beautiful family, wealth, and influence. But at night, he would wake up choking, seeing hooded figures, and hearing incantations in his dreams. His grandfather had been a 33rd-degree Mason, and Jason still wore the ring.

He once jokingly said the Masonic vows at a club event — but the moment he did, **something entered him**. His mind began breaking down. He heard voices. His wife left him. He tried to end it all.

At a retreat, someone discerned the Masonic link. Jason wept as he **renounced every oath**, broke the ring, and underwent deliverance for three hours. That night, for the first time in years, he slept in peace.

His testimony?

"You don't joke with secret altars. They speak — until you make them shut up in Jesus' name."

GLOBAL WEB OF THE BROTHERHOOD

- **Europe** – Freemasonry deeply embedded in business, politics, and church denominations.
- **Africa** – Illuminati and secret orders offering wealth in exchange for souls; cults in universities.
- **Latin America** – Jesuit infiltration and Masonic rites mixed with Catholic mysticism.
- **Asia** – Ancient mystery schools, temple priesthoods tied to generational oaths.
- **North America** – Eastern Star, Scottish Rite, fraternities like Skull & Bones, Bohemian Grove elites.

These cults often invoke "God," but not the **God of the Bible** — they reference the **Great Architect**, an impersonal force tied to **Luciferian light**.

Signs You're Affected

- Chronic illness that doctors can't explain.
- Fear of advancement or fear of breaking from family systems.
- Dreams of robes, rituals, secret doors, lodges, or strange ceremonies.
- Depression or insanity in the male line.
- Women struggling with barrenness, abuse, or fear.

Deliverance Action Plan

1. **Renounce all known oaths** – especially if you or your family were part of Freemasonry, Rosicrucians, Eastern Star, Kabala, or any "brotherhood."
2. **Break every degree** – from Entered Apprentice to 33rd Degree, by name.
3. **Destroy all symbols** – rings, aprons, books, pendants, certificates,

etc.

4. **Close the gate** – spiritually and legally through prayer and declaration.

Use these scriptures:

- Isaiah 28:18 — "Your covenant with death shall be annulled."
- Galatians 3:13 — "Christ redeemed us from the curse of the law."
- Ezekiel 13:20–23 — "I will tear your veils and free My people."

Group Application

- Ask if any member had parents or grandparents in secret societies.
- Lead a **guided renunciation** through all degrees of Freemasonry (you can create a printed script for this).
- Use symbolic acts — burn an old ring or draw a cross over the forehead to nullify the "third eye" opened in rituals.
- Pray over minds, necks, and backs — these are common sites of bondage.

Key Insight
Brotherhood without the blood of Christ is a brotherhood of bondage.
You must choose: covenant with man or covenant with God.
Reflection Journal

- Has anyone in my family been involved in Freemasonry, mysticism, or secret oaths?
- Have I unknowingly recited or mimicked vows, creeds, or symbols tied to secret societies?
- Am I willing to break family tradition to walk fully in God's covenant?

Prayer of Renunciation
Father, in the name of Jesus, I renounce every covenant, oath, or ritual tied to Freemasonry, Kabbalah, or any secret society — in my life or

bloodline. I break every degree, every lie, every demonic right that was granted through ceremonies or symbols. I declare that Jesus Christ is my only Light, my only Architect, and my only Lord. I receive freedom now, in Jesus' name. Amen.

DAY 35: WITCHES IN THE PEWS — WHEN EVIL ENTERS THROUGH THE CHURCH DOORS

"*For such men are false apostles, deceitful workmen, disguising themselves as apostles of Christ. And no wonder, for even Satan disguises himself as an angel of light.*" — 2 Corinthians 11:13–14

"*I know your deeds, your love and faith… Nevertheless, I have this against you: You tolerate that woman Jezebel, who calls herself a prophetess…*" — Revelation 2:19–20

The most dangerous witch is not the one flying at night.

It's the one **sitting next to you in church**.

They don't wear black robes or ride broomsticks.

They lead prayer meetings.

Sing on worship teams.

Prophesy in tongues.

Pastor churches.

And yet… they are **carriers of darkness**.

Some know exactly what they're doing — sent as spiritual assassins.

Others are victims of ancestral witchcraft or rebellion, operating with gifts that are **unclean**.

The Church As Cover — "Miriam's" Story

Miriam was a popular deliverance minister in a large West African church. Her voice commanded demons to flee. People traveled across nations to be anointed by her.

But Miriam had a secret: at night, she traveled out of her body. She would see church members' homes, their weaknesses, and their bloodlines. She thought it was the "prophetic."

Her power grew. But so did her torment.

She began hearing voices. Couldn't sleep. Her children were attacked. Her husband left her.

She finally confessed: she had been "activated" as a child by her grandmother, a powerful witch who made her sleep under cursed blankets.

"I thought I was filled with the Holy Spirit. It was a spirit... but not Holy."

She went through deliverance. But the warfare has never stopped. She says:

"If I hadn't confessed, I would have died on an altar in fire... in church."

Global Situations of Hidden Witchcraft in the Church

- **Africa** – Spiritual envy. Prophets using divination, rituals, water spirits. Many altars are actually portals.
- **Europe** – Psychic mediums masquerading as "spiritual coaches." Witchcraft wrapped in new age Christianity.
- **Asia** – Temple priestesses entering churches to plant curses and astral-monitor converts.
- **Latin America** – Santería-practicing "pastors" who preach deliverance but sacrifice chickens at night.
- **North America** – Christian witches claiming "Jesus and tarot," energy healers on church stages, and pastors involved in Freemasonry rites.

Signs of Witchcraft Operating in the Church

- Heavy atmosphere or confusion during worship.
- Dreams of snakes, sex, or animals after services.
- Leadership falling into sudden sin or scandal.
- "Prophecies" that manipulate, seduce, or shame.
- Anyone who says "God told me you're my husband/wife."
- Strange objects found near the pulpit or altars.

DELIVERANCE ACTION Plan

1. **Pray for discernment** — Ask the Holy Spirit to reveal if there are

hidden witches in your fellowship.
2. **Test every spirit** — Even if they sound spiritual (1 John 4:1).
3. **Break soul ties** — If you've been prayed over, prophesied to, or touched by someone unclean, **renounce it**.
4. **Pray over your church** — Declare the fire of God to expose every hidden altar, secret sin, and spiritual leech.
5. **If you're a victim** — Get help. Don't stay silent or alone.

Group Application

- Ask group members: Have you ever felt uncomfortable or spiritually violated in a church service?
- Lead a **corporate cleansing prayer** for the fellowship.
- Anoint every person and declare a **spiritual firewall** around minds, altars, and gifts.
- Teach leaders how to **screen gifts** and **test spirits** before allowing people into visible roles.

Key Insight
Not all who say "Lord, Lord" are from the Lord.
The church is the **prime battlefield** for spiritual contamination — but also the place of healing when truth is upheld.

Reflection Journal

- Have I received prayers, impartations, or mentorship from someone whose life bore unholy fruit?
- Are there times I felt "off" after church, but ignored it?
- Am I willing to confront witchcraft even if it wears a suit or sings on stage?

Prayer of Exposure and Freedom
Lord Jesus, I thank You for being the true Light. I ask You now to expose every hidden agent of darkness operating in or around my life and fellowship. I renounce every unholy impartation, false prophecy, or soul tie I've received from spiritual impostors. Cleanse me with Your blood. Purify

my gifts. Guard my gates. Burn away every counterfeit spirit with Your holy fire. In Jesus' name. Amen.

DAY 36: CODED SPELLS — WHEN SONGS, FASHION & MOVIES BECOME PORTALS

"*Take no part in the unfruitful works of darkness, but instead expose them.*" — Ephesians 5:11

"*Have nothing to do with godless myths and old wives' tales; rather, train yourself to be godly.*" — 1 Timothy 4:7

Not every battle begins with a blood sacrifice.

Some begin with a **beat**.

A melody.

A catchy lyric that sticks in your soul.

Or a **symbol** on your clothes you thought was "cool."

Or a "harmless" show you binge while demons smile in the shadows.

In today's hyper-connected world, witchcraft is **coded** — hiding in **plain sight** through media, music, movies, and fashion.

A Darkened Sound — Real Story: "The Headphones"

Elijah, a 17-year-old in the U.S., started having panic attacks, sleepless nights, and demonic dreams. His Christian parents thought it was stress.

But during a deliverance session, the Holy Spirit instructed the team to ask about his **music**.

He confessed: "I listen to trap metal. I know it's dark... but it helps me feel powerful."

When the team played one of his favorite songs in prayer, a **manifestation** occurred.

The beats were encoded with **chant tracks** from occult rituals. Backwards masking revealed phrases like "submit your soul" and "Lucifer speaks."

Once Elijah deleted the music, repented, and renounced the connection, peace returned.

The war had entered through his **ear gates**.

Global Programming Patterns

- **Africa** – Afrobeat songs tied to money rituals; "juju" references hidden in lyrics; fashion brands with marine kingdom symbols.
- **Asia** – K-pop with subliminal sexual and spirit-channeling messages; anime characters infused with Shinto demon lore.
- **Latin America** – Reggaeton pushing Santería chants and backward-coded spells.
- **Europe** – Fashion houses (Gucci, Balenciaga) embedding satanic imagery and rituals into runway culture.
- **North America** – Hollywood films coded with witchcraft (Marvel, horror, "light vs dark" movies); cartoons using spellcasting as fun.

Common Entry Portals (and Their Spirit Assignments)

Media Type	Portal	Demonic Assignment
Music	Beats/samples from rituals	Torment, violence, rebellion
TV Series	Magic, lust, murder glorification	Desensitization, soul dulling
Fashion	Symbols (serpent, eye, goat, triangles)	Identity confusion, spiritual binding
Video Games	Sorcery, blood rites, avatars	Astral transfer, addiction, occult alignment
Social Media	Trends on "manifestation," crystals, spells	Sorcery normalization

ACTION PLAN – DISCERN, Detox, Defend

1. **Audit your playlist, wardrobe, and watch history.** Look for occult,

lustful, rebellious, or violent content.
2. **Ask the Holy Spirit to expose** every unholy influence.
3. **Delete and destroy**. Don't sell or donate. Burn or trash anything demonic — physical or digital.
4. **Anoint your devices**, room, and ears. Declare them sanctified for God's glory.
5. **Replace with truth**: Worship music, godly films, books, and Scripture readings that renew your mind.

Group Application

- Lead members in a "Media Inventory." Let each person write down shows, songs, or items they suspect may be portals.
- Pray over phones and headphones. Anoint them.
- Do a group "detox fast" — 3 to 7 days with no secular media. Only feed on God's Word, worship, and fellowship.
- Testify the results at the next meeting.

Key Insight
Demons no longer need a shrine to enter your house. All they need is your consent to press play.

Reflection Journal

- What have I watched, heard, or worn that might be an open door to oppression?
- Am I willing to give up what entertains me if it's also enslaving me?
- Have I normalized rebellion, lust, violence, or mockery in the name of "art"?

PRAYER OF PURGING

Lord Jesus, I come before You asking for full spiritual detox. Expose every coded spell I've let into my life through music, fashion, games, or media. I repent of watching, wearing, and listening to what dishonors You. Today, I sever the soul ties. I cast out every spirit of rebellion, witchcraft, lust, confusion, or torment. Cleanse my eyes, ears, and heart. I now dedicate my body, media, and choices to You alone. In Jesus' name. Amen.

DAY 37: THE INVISIBLE ALTARS OF POWER — FREEMASONS, KABBALAH, & OCCULT ELITES

"*Again, the devil took Him to a very high mountain and showed Him all the kingdoms of the world and their splendor. 'All this I will give You,' he said, 'if You will bow down and worship me.'*" — Matthew 4:8–9

"*You cannot drink the cup of the Lord and the cup of demons too; you cannot have a part in both the Lord's table and the table of demons.*" — 1 Corinthians 10:21

There are altars hidden not in caves, but in boardrooms.

Spirits not just in jungles — but in government halls, financial towers, Ivy League libraries, and sanctuaries disguised as "churches."

Welcome to the realm of the **elite occult**:

Freemasons, Rosicrucians, Kabballists, Jesuit orders, Eastern Stars, and hidden Luciferian priesthoods who **cloak their devotion to Satan in ritual, secrecy, and symbols.** Their gods are reason, power, and ancient knowledge — but their **souls are pledged to the darkness.**

Hidden in Plain Sight

- **Freemasonry** cloaks itself as a fraternity of builders — yet its higher degrees invoke demonic entities, swear death oaths, and exalt Lucifer as "light-bearer."
- **Kabbalah** promises mystical access to God — but it subtly replaces Yahweh with cosmic energy maps and numerology.
- **Jesuit mysticism**, in its corrupted forms, often blends Catholic imagery with spiritual manipulation and control of world systems.
- **Hollywood, Fashion, Finance, & Politics** all carry coded messages, symbols, and **public rituals that are really worship services to**

Lucifer.

You don't need to be a celebrity to be affected. These systems **pollute nations** through:

- Media programming
- Educational systems
- Religious compromise
- Financial dependency
- Rituals disguised as "initiations," "pledges," or "brand deals"

True Story – "The Lodge Ruined My Lineage"
Solomon (name changed), a successful business magnate from the UK, joined a Masonic lodge for networking. He rose quickly, gaining wealth and prestige. But he also started having terrifying nightmares — cloaked men summoning him, blood oaths, dark animals chasing him. His daughter began cutting herself, claiming a "presence" made her do it.

One night, he saw a man in his room — half-human, half-jackal — who told him: *"You are mine. The price has been paid."* He reached out to a deliverance ministry. It took **seven months of renunciation, fasting, vomiting rituals, and replacing every occult tie** — before peace came.

He later discovered: **His grandfather was a 33rd-degree mason. He had only continued the legacy unknowingly.**

Global Reach

- **Africa** – Secret societies among tribal rulers, judges, pastors — swearing allegiance to blood oaths in exchange for power.
- **Europe** – Knights of Malta, Illuminist lodges, and elite esoteric universities.
- **North America** – Masonic foundations under most founding documents, court structures, and even churches.
- **Asia** – Hidden dragon cults, ancestral orders, and political groups rooted in Buddhism-shamanism hybrids.
- **Latin America** – Syncretic cults blending Catholic saints with Luciferian spirits like Santa Muerte or Baphomet.

Action Plan — Escaping Elite Altars

1. **Renounce** any involvement in Freemasonry, Eastern Star, Jesuit oaths, Gnostic books, or mystic systems — even "academic" study of such.
2. **Destroy** regalia, rings, pins, books, aprons, photos, and symbols.
3. **Break word curses** — especially death oaths and initiation vows. Use Isaiah 28:18 ("Your covenant with death will be annulled…").
4. **Fast 3 days** while reading Ezekiel 8, Isaiah 47, and Revelation 17.
5. **Replace the altar**: Rededicate yourself to the altar of Christ alone (Romans 12:1–2). Communion. Worship. Anointing.

You can't be in the courts of heaven and in the courts of Lucifer at the same time. Choose your altar.

Group Application

- Map out common elite organizations in your region — and pray directly against their spiritual influence.
- Hold a session where members can confidentially confess if their families were involved in Freemasonry or similar cults.
- Bring oil and communion — lead a mass renunciation of oaths, rituals, and seals made in secret.
- Break pride — remind the group: **No access is worth your soul.**

Key Insight

Secret societies promise light. But only Jesus is the Light of the World. Every other altar demands blood — but cannot save.

Reflection Journal

- Was anyone in my bloodline involved in secret societies or "orders"?
- Have I read or owned occult books masked as academic texts?
- What symbols (pentagrams, all-seeing eyes, suns, serpents, pyramids) are hidden in my clothing, art, or jewelry?

Prayer of Renunciation

Father, I renounce every secret society, lodge, oath, ritual, or altar not founded on Jesus Christ. I break the covenants of my fathers, my bloodline, and my own mouth. I reject Freemasonry, Kabbalah, mysticism, and every hidden pact made for power. I destroy every symbol, every seal, and every lie that promised light but delivered bondage. Jesus, I enthrone You again as my only Master. Shine Your light into every secret place. In Your name, I walk free. Amen.

DAY 38: WOMB COVENANTS & WATER KINGDOMS — WHEN DESTINY IS DEFILED BEFORE BIRTH

"*The wicked are estranged from the womb; they go astray as soon as they are born, speaking lies.*" — Psalm 58:3

"*Before I formed you in the womb I knew you, before you were born I set you apart...*" — Jeremiah 1:5

What if the battles you're fighting didn't start with your choices — but your conception?

What if your name was spoken in dark places while you were still in the womb?

What if **your identity was exchanged**, your **destiny sold**, and your **soul marked** — before you took your first breath?

This is the reality of **underwater initiation**, **marine spirit covenants**, and **occult womb claims** that **bind generations**, especially in regions with deep ancestral and coastal rituals.

The Water Kingdom — Satan's Throne Below

In the unseen realm, Satan rules **more than just the air**. He also governs **the marine world** — a vast demonic network of spirits, altars, and rituals under oceans, rivers, and lakes.

Marine spirits (commonly called *Mami Wata, Queen of the Coast, spirit wives/husbands*, etc.) are responsible for:

- Premature death
- Barrenness and miscarriages
- Sexual bondage and dreams
- Mental torment
- Afflictions in newborns

- Business rise-and-crash patterns

But how do these spirits gain **legal ground**?
At the womb.
Unseen Initiations Before Birth

- **Ancestral dedications** – A child "promised" to a deity if born healthy.
- **Occult priestesses** touching the womb during pregnancy.
- **Covenant names** given by family — unknowingly honoring marine queens or spirits.
- **Birth rituals** done with river water, charms, or herbs from shrines.
- **Umbilical cord burial** with incantations.
- **Pregnancy in occult environments** (e.g., Freemasonry lodges, new age centers, polygamous cults).

Some children are born already enslaved. That's why they scream violently at birth — their spirit senses darkness.

Real Story – "My Baby Belonged to the River"

Jessica, from Sierra Leone, had been trying to conceive for 5 years. Finally, she got pregnant after a "prophet" gave her a soap to bathe with and an oil to rub on her womb. The baby was born strong — but by 3 months old, began crying nonstop, always at night. He hated water, screamed during baths, and would shake uncontrollably when taken near the river.

One day, her son convulsed and died for 4 minutes. He revived — and **started speaking in full words at 9 months**: "I don't belong here. I belong to the Queen."

Terrified, Jessica sought deliverance. The child was only released after 14 days of fasting and renunciation prayers — her husband had to destroy a family idol hidden in his village before the torment stopped.

Babies are not born blank. They're born into battles we must fight on their behalf.

GLOBAL PARALLELS

- **Africa** – River altars, Mami Wata dedications, placenta rituals.
- **Asia** – Water spirits invoked during Buddhist or animist births.
- **Europe** – Druidic midwife covenants, ancestral water rites, freemasonic dedications.
- **Latin America** – Santeria naming, spirits of rivers (e.g., Oshun), birth under astrology charts.
- **North America** – New age birthing rituals, hypno-birthing with spirit guides, "blessing ceremonies" by mediums.

Signs of Womb-Initiated Bondage

- Repeating miscarriage patterns across generations
- Night terrors in infants and children
- Unexplained infertility despite medical clearance
- Constant water dreams (oceans, floods, swimming, mermaids)
- Irrational fear of water or drowning
- Feeling "claimed" — as if something is watching from birth

Action Plan — Break the Womb Covenant

1. **Ask the Holy Spirit** to reveal if you (or your child) were initiated through womb rituals.
2. **Renounce** any covenant made during pregnancy — knowingly or unknowingly.
3. **Pray over your own birth story** — even if your mother is unavailable, speak as the legal spiritual gatekeeper of your life.
4. **Fast with Isaiah 49 and Psalm 139** – to reclaim your divine blueprint.
5. **If pregnant**: Anoint your belly and speak daily over your unborn child:

"You are set apart for the Lord. No spirit of water, blood, or darkness shall own you. You belong to Jesus Christ — body, soul, and spirit."

Group Application

- Ask participants to write down what they know about their birth story — including rituals, midwives, or naming events.
- Encourage parents to dedicate their children afresh in a "Christ-Centered Naming & Covenant Service."
- Lead prayers breaking water covenants using *Isaiah 28:18*, *Colossians 2:14*, and *Revelation 12:11*.

Key Insight

The womb is a gate — and what passes through it often enters with spiritual baggage. But no womb altar is greater than the Cross.

Reflection Journal

- Were there any objects, oils, charms, or names involved in my conception or birth?
- Do I experience spiritual attacks that began in childhood?
- Have I unknowingly passed down marine covenants to my children?

Prayer of Release

Heavenly Father, You knew me before I was formed. Today I break every hidden covenant, water ritual, and demonic dedication done at or before my birth. I reject every claim of marine spirits, familiar spirits, or generational womb altars. Let the blood of Jesus rewrite my birth story and the story of my children. I am born of the Spirit — not of water altars. In Jesus' name. Amen.

DAY 39: WATER BAPTIZED INTO BONDAGE — HOW INFANTS, INITIALS & UNSEEN COVENANTS OPEN DOORS

"*They poured out innocent blood, the blood of their sons and daughters, whom they sacrificed to the idols of Canaan, and the land was desecrated by their blood.*" — Psalm 106:38

"*Can plunder be taken from warriors, or captives be rescued from the fierce?* But this is what the Lord says: *Yes, captives will be taken from warriors, and plunder retrieved from the fierce...*" — Isaiah 49:24–25

Many destinies were not just **derailed in adulthood** — they were **hijacked in infancy**.

That seemingly innocent naming ceremony...

That casual dip in river water "to bless the child"...

The coin in the hand...

The cut under the tongue...

The oil from a "spiritual grandmother"...

Even the initials given at birth...

They may all seem cultural. Traditional. Harmless.

But the kingdom of darkness **hides in tradition**, and many children have been **secretly initiated** before they could ever say "Jesus."

Real Story – "I Was Named by the River"

In Haiti, a boy named Malick grew up with a strange fear of rivers and storms. As a toddler, he was taken by his grandmother to a stream to be "introduced to the spirits" for protection. He began hearing voices by age 7. At 10, he had night visitations. By 14, he attempted suicide after feeling a "presence" always by his side.

At a deliverance meeting, the demons manifested violently, screaming, "We entered at the river! We were called by name!" His name, "Malick," had been part of a spiritual naming tradition to "honor the river queen." Until he was renamed in Christ, torment continued. He now ministers in deliverance among youth caught in ancestral dedications.

How It Happens — The Hidden Traps

1. **Initials as Covenants**
   Some initials, especially those tied to ancestral names, family gods, or water deities (e.g., "M.M." = Mami/Marine; "O.L." = Oya/Orisha Lineage), act as demonic signatures.
2. **Infant Dips in Rivers/Streams**
   Done "for protection" or "cleansing," these are often **baptisms into marine spirits.**
3. **Secret Naming Ceremonies**
   Where another name (different from the public one) is whispered or spoken before an altar or shrine.
4. **Birthmark Rituals**
   Oils, ash, or blood placed on foreheads or limbs to "mark" a child for spirits.
5. **Water-Fed Umbilical Cord Burials**
   Umbilical cords dropped into rivers, streams, or buried with water incantations—tying the child to water altars.

If your parents didn't covenant you to Christ, chances are someone else claimed you.

Global Occult Womb-Bonding Practices

- **Africa** – Naming babies after river deities, burying cords near marine altars.
- **Caribbean/Latin America** – Santeria baptism rituals, Yoruba-style dedications with herbs and river items.
- **Asia** – Hindu rituals involving Ganges water, astrologically calculated naming tied to elemental spirits.
- **Europe** – Druidic or esoteric naming traditions invoking forest/water guardians.

- **North America** – Native ritual dedications, modern Wicca baby blessings, new age naming ceremonies invoking "ancient guides."

How Do I Know?

- Unexplained early childhood torment, illnesses, or "imaginary friends"
- Dreams of rivers, mermaids, being chased by water
- Aversion to churches but fascination with mystical things
- A deep sense of "being followed" or watched from birth
- Discovering a second name or unknown ceremony tied to your infancy

Action Plan – Redeem the Infancy

1. **Ask the Holy Spirit**: What happened when I was born? What spiritual hands touched me?
2. **Renounce all hidden dedications**, even if done in ignorance: "I reject any covenant made on my behalf that was not to the Lord Jesus Christ."
3. **Break ties to ancestral names, initials, and tokens**.
4. **Use Isaiah 49:24–26, Colossians 2:14, and 2 Corinthians 5:17** to declare identity in Christ.
5. If needed, **hold a re-dedication ceremony** — present yourself (or your children) to God anew, and declare new names if led.

GROUP APPLICATION

- Invite participants to research the story of their names.
- Create a space for spiritual re-naming if led — allow people to claim names like "David," "Esther," or spirit-led identities.
- Lead the group in a symbolic *re-baptism* of dedication — not water immersion, but anointing and word-based covenant with Christ.

- Have parents break covenants over their children in prayer: "You belong to Jesus — no spirit, river, or ancestral tie has any legal ground."

Key Insight

Your beginning matters. But it doesn't have to define your end. Every river claim can be broken by the river of the blood of Jesus.

Reflection Journal

- What names or initials were I given, and what do they mean?
- Were there secret or cultural rituals done at my birth I need to renounce?
- Have I truly dedicated my life — my body, soul, name, and identity — to the Lord Jesus Christ?

Prayer of Redemption

Father God, I come before You in the name of Jesus. I renounce every covenant, dedication, and ritual done at my birth. I reject every naming, water initiation, and ancestral claim. Whether through initials, naming, or hidden altars — I cancel every demonic right to my life. I now declare that I am fully Yours. My name is written in the Book of Life. My past is covered by the blood of Jesus, and my identity is sealed by the Holy Spirit. Amen.

DAY 40: FROM DELIVERED TO DELIVERER — YOUR PAIN IS YOUR ORDINATION

"*But the people that do know their God shall be strong, and do exploits.*" — Daniel 11:32

"*Then the Lord raised up judges, who saved them out of the hands of these raiders.*" — Judges 2:16

You were not delivered to sit quietly in church.

You were not set free just to survive.

You were delivered **to deliver others**.

The same Jesus who healed the demoniac in Mark 5 sent him back to Decapolis to tell the story. No seminary. No ordination. Just a **burning testimony** and a mouth set on fire.

You are that man. That woman. That family. That nation.

The pain you've endured is now your weapon.

The torment you escaped is your trumpet.

What held you in darkness now becomes the **stage of your dominion.**

Real Story – From Marine Bride to Deliverance Minister

Rebecca, from Cameroon, was a former bride of a marine spirit. She was initiated at age 8 during a coastal naming ceremony. By 16, she was having sex in dreams, controlling men with her eyes, and had caused multiple divorces through sorcery. She was known as "the pretty curse."

When she encountered the gospel in university, her demons went wild. It took six months of fasting, deliverance, and deep discipleship before she was free.

Today, she holds deliverance conferences for women across Africa. Thousands have been freed through her obedience.

What if she had remained silent?

Apostolic Rise — Global Deliverers Are Being Born

- **In Africa**, ex-witchdoctors now plant churches.
- **In Asia**, ex-Buddhists preach Christ in secret houses.
- **In Latin America**, former Santeria priests now break altars.
- **In Europe**, ex-occultists lead expository Bible studies online.
- **In North America**, survivors of new age deceptions are leading deliverance Zooms weekly.

They are **the unlikelies**, the broken ones, the former slaves of darkness now marching in light — and **you are one of them**.

Final Action Plan – Step Into Your Call

1. **Write your testimony** — even if you feel it's not dramatic. Someone needs your freedom story.
2. **Start small** — Pray for a friend. Host a Bible study. Share your deliverance process.
3. **Never stop learning** — Deliverers stay in the Word, stay repentant, and stay sharp.
4. **Cover your family** — Declare daily that the darkness stops with you and your children.
5. **Declare spiritual war zones** — Your workplace, your home, your street. Be the gatekeeper.

Group Commissioning
Today is not just a devotion — it's a **commissioning ceremony**.

- Anoint each other's heads with oil and say:

"You are delivered to deliver. Arise, Judge of God."

- Declare aloud as a group:

"We are no longer survivors. We are warriors. We carry light, and darkness trembles."

- Appoint prayer pairings or accountability partners to continue growing in boldness and impact.

Key Insight
The greatest revenge against the kingdom of darkness is not just freedom. It is multiplication.

Final Reflection Journal

- What was the moment I knew I had crossed from darkness into light?
- Who needs to hear my story?
- Where can I begin to shine light intentionally this week?
- Am I willing to be mocked, misunderstood, and resisted — for the sake of setting others free?

Prayer of Commissioning
Father God, I thank You for 40 days of fire, freedom, and truth. You did not save me just to shelter me — You delivered me to deliver others. Today, I receive this mantle. My testimony is a sword. My scars are weapons. My prayers are hammers. My obedience is worship. I now walk in the name of Jesus — as a firestarter, a deliverer, a light-bearer. I am Yours. The darkness has no place in me, and no place around me. I take my place. In Jesus' name. Amen.

360° DAILY DECLARATION OF DELIVERANCE & DOMINION – Part 1

"*No weapon formed against you shall prosper, and every tongue which rises against you in judgment you shall condemn. This is the heritage of the servants of the Lord...*" — Isaiah 54:17

Today and every day, I take my full position in Christ — spirit, soul, and body.

I close every door — known and unknown — to the kingdom of darkness.

I break all contact, contract, covenant, or communion with evil altars, ancestral spirits, spirit spouses, occult societies, witchcraft, and demonic alliances — by the blood of Jesus!

I declare I am not for sale. I am not accessible. I am not recruitable. I am not re-initiated.

Every satanic recall, spiritual surveillance, or evil summoning — be scattered by fire, in the name of Jesus!

I bind myself to the mind of Christ, the will of the Father, and the voice of the Holy Spirit.

I walk in light, in truth, in power, in purity, and in purpose.

I shut every third eye, psychic gate, and unholy portal opened through dreams, trauma, sex, rituals, media, or false teachings.

Let the fire of God consume every illegal deposit in my soul, in Jesus' name.

I speak to the air, land, sea, stars, and heavens — you will not work against me.

Every hidden altar, agent, watcher, or whispering demon assigned against my life, family, calling, or territory — be disarmed and silenced by the blood of Jesus!

I soak my mind in the Word of God.

I declare my dreams are sanctified.

My thoughts are shielded.
My sleep is holy.
My body is a temple of fire.
From this moment forward, I walk in 360-degree deliverance — nothing hidden, nothing missed.
Every lingering bondage breaks.
Every generational yoke shatters.
Every unrepented sin is exposed and cleansed.
I declare:

- **Darkness has no dominion over me.**
- **My home is a fire zone.**
- **My gates are sealed in glory.**
- **I live in obedience and walk in power.**

I arise as a deliverer to my generation.
I will not look back. I will not go back.
I am light. I am fire. I am free.
In Jesus' mighty name. Amen!

360° DAILY DECLARATION OF DELIVERANCE & DOMINION – Part 2

Protection from witchcraft, sorcery, necromancers, mediums, and demonic channels

Deliverance for yourself and others under their influence or bondage

Cleansing and covering through the blood of Jesus

Restoration of soundness, identity, and freedom in Christ

Protection and Freedom from Witchcraft, Mediums, Necromancers, and Spiritual Bondage

(Through the Blood of Jesus and the Word of Our Testimony)

"And they overcame him by the blood of the Lamb, and by the word of their testimony..."

— *Revelation 12:11*

"The Lord ... foils the signs of false prophets and makes fools of diviners ... confirms the word of His servant and fulfills the counsel of His messengers."

— *Isaiah 44:25–26*

"The Spirit of the Lord is upon me... to proclaim liberty to the captives and release to those who are bound..."

— *Luke 4:18*

OPENING PRAYER:

Father God, I come boldly today by the blood of Jesus. I acknowledge the power in Your name and declare that You alone are my deliverer and defender. I stand as Your servant and witness, and I declare Your Word with boldness and authority today.

DECLARATIONS OF PROTECTION AND DELIVERANCE

1. **Deliverance from Witchcraft, Mediums, Necromancers, and Spiritual Influence:**

- I **break and renounce** every curse, spell, divination, enchantment, manipulation, monitoring, astral projection, or soul tie—spoken or enacted—through witchcraft, necromancy, mediums, or spiritual channels.
- I **declare** that the **blood of Jesus** is against every unclean spirit that seeks to bind, distract, deceive, or manipulate me or my family.
- I command **all spiritual interference, possession, oppression, or soul bondage** to be broken now by the authority in the name of Jesus Christ.
- I speak **deliverance for myself and for every person knowingly or unknowingly under the influence of witchcraft or false light**. Come out now! Be free, in Jesus' name!
- I call upon the fire of God to **burn every spiritual yoke, satanic contract, and altar** erected in the spirit to enslave or ensnare our destinies.

"There is no enchantment against Jacob, no divination against Israel." — *Numbers 23:23*

2. **Cleansing and Protection of Self, Children, and Family:**

- I plead the blood of Jesus over my **mind, soul, spirit, body, emotions, family, children, and work.**
- I declare: I and my house are **sealed by the Holy Spirit and hidden with Christ in God.**
- No weapon formed against us shall prosper. Every tongue speaking evil against us is **judged and silenced** in Jesus' name.
- I renounce and cast out every **spirit of fear, torment, confusion, seduction, or control**.

"I am the LORD, who frustrates the tokens of the liars..." — *Isaiah 44:25*

3. **Restoration of Identity, Purpose, and Sound Mind:**

- I reclaim every part of my soul and identity that was **traded, trapped, or stolen** through deception or spiritual compromise.
- I declare: I have the **mind of Christ**, and I walk in clarity, wisdom, and authority.
- I declare: I am **delivered from every generational curse and household witchcraft**, and I walk in covenant with the Lord.

"God has not given me a spirit of fear, but of power, love, and a sound mind." — *2 Timothy 1:7*

4. Daily Covering and Victory in Christ:

- I declare: Today, I walk in divine **protection, discernment, and peace**.
- The blood of Jesus speaks **better things** for me—protection, healing, authority, and freedom.
- Every evil assignment set for this day is overturned. I walk in victory and triumph in Christ Jesus.

"A thousand may fall at my side and ten thousand at my right hand, but it shall not come near me..." — *Psalm 91:7*

FINAL DECLARATION AND TESTIMONY:

"I overcome every form of darkness, witchcraft, necromancy, sorcery, psychic manipulation, soul tampering, and evil spiritual transfer—not by my strength but **by the blood of Jesus and the Word of my testimony**."

"I declare: **I am delivered. My household is delivered.** Every hidden yoke is broken. Every trap is exposed. Every false light is extinguished. I walk in liberty. I walk in truth. I walk in the power of the Holy Spirit."

"The Lord confirms the word of His servant and performs the counsel of His messenger. So shall it be this day and every day henceforth."

In Jesus' mighty name, **Amen.**

SCRIPTURE REFERENCES:

- Isaiah 44:24–26
- Revelation 12:11
- Isaiah 54:17

- Psalm 91
- Numbers 23:23
- Luke 4:18
- Ephesians 6:10–18
- Colossians 3:3
- 2 Timothy 1:7

360° DAILY DECLARATION OF DELIVERANCE & DOMINION - Part 3

"*The Lord is a man of war: the Lord is His name.*" — Exodus 15:3

"*They overcame him by the blood of the Lamb and by the word of their testimony...*" — Revelation 12:11

Today, I arise and take my place in Christ — seated in heavenly places, far above all principalities, powers, thrones, dominions, and every name that is named.

I RENOUNCE

I renounce every known and unknown covenant, oath, or initiation:

- Freemasonry (1st to 33rd degrees)
- Kabbala and Jewish mysticism
- Eastern Star and Rosicrucians
- Jesuit orders and Illuminati
- Satanic brotherhoods and Luciferian sects
- Marine spirits and undersea covenants
- Kundalini serpents, chakra alignments, and third-eye activations
- New Age deception, Reiki, Christian yoga, and astral travel
- Witchcraft, sorcery, necromancy, and astral contracts
- Occult soul ties from sex, rituals, and secret pacts
- Masonic oaths over my bloodline and ancestral priesthoods

I sever every spiritual umbilical cord to:

- Ancient blood altars
- False prophetic fire
- Spirit spouses and dream invaders
- Sacred geometry, light codes, and universal law doctrines

- False christs, familiar spirits, and counterfeit holy spirits

Let the blood of Jesus speak on my behalf. Let every contract be torn. Let every altar be shattered. Let every demonic identity be erased — now!

I DECLARE
I declare:

- My body is a living temple of the Holy Spirit.
- My mind is guarded by the helmet of salvation.
- My soul is sanctified daily by the washing of the Word.
- My blood is cleansed by Calvary.
- My dreams are sealed in light.
- My name is written in the Lamb's Book of Life — not in any occult registry, lodge, logbook, scroll, or seal!

I COMMAND
I command:

- Every agent of darkness — watchers, monitors, astral projectors — to be blinded and scattered.
- Every tether to the underworld, the marine world, and the astral plane — be broken!
- Every dark mark, implant, ritual wound, or spiritual branding — be purged by fire!
- Every familiar spirit whispering lies — be silenced now!

I DISENGAGE
I disengage from:

- All demonic timelines, soul prisons, and spirit cages
- All secret society rankings and degrees
- All false mantles, thrones, or crowns I've worn
- Every identity not authored by God
- Every alliance, friendship, or relationship empowered by dark systems

I ESTABLISH

I establish:

- A firewall of glory around me and my household
- Holy angels at every gate, portal, window, and pathway
- Purity in my media, music, memories, and mind
- Truth in my friendships, ministry, marriage, and mission
- Unbroken communion with the Holy Spirit

I SUBMIT

I submit myself wholly to Jesus Christ —
The Lamb that was slain, the King that rules, the Lion that roars.
I choose light. I choose truth. I choose obedience.
I don't belong to the dark kingdoms of this world.
I belong to the Kingdom of our God and of His Christ.

I WARN THE ENEMY

By this declaration I issue notice to:

- Every high-ranking principality
- Every ruling spirit over cities, bloodlines, and nations
- Every astral traveler, witch, warlock, or fallen star…

I am untouchable property.
My name is not found in your archives.
My soul is not for sale.
My dreams are under command.
My body is not your temple.
My future is not your playground.
I will not return to bondage.
I will not repeat ancestral cycles.
I will not carry strange fire.
I will not be a resting place for serpents.

I SEAL

I seal this declaration with:

- The blood of Jesus
- The fire of the Holy Ghost
- The authority of the Word
- The unity of the Body of Christ
- The sound of my testimony

In Jesus name, Amen and Amen

CONCLUSION: FROM SURVIVAL TO SONSHIP — STAYING FREE, LIVING FREE, SETTING OTHERS FREE

"*Stand fast therefore in the liberty wherewith Christ hath made us free, and be not entangled again with the yoke of bondage.*" — Galatians 5:1

"*He brought them out of darkness and the shadow of death, and broke their chains in pieces.*" — Psalm 107:14

These 40 days were never just about knowledge. They were about **warfare**, **awakening**, and **walking in dominion**.

You've seen how the dark kingdom operates — subtly, generationally, sometimes openly. You've journeyed through ancestral gates, dream realms, occultic pacts, global rituals, and spiritual torment. You've encountered testimonies of unimaginable pain — but also **radical deliverance**. You've broken altars, renounced lies, and confronted things many pulpits are too afraid to name.

BUT THIS IS NOT THE END.

Now begins the real journey: **Maintaining your freedom. Living in the Spirit. Teaching others the way out.**

It's easy to go through 40 days of fire and return to Egypt. It's easy to tear down altars only to rebuild them in loneliness, lust, or spiritual fatigue.

Don't.

You are no longer a **slave to cycles**. You are a **watchman** on the wall. A **gatekeeper** for your family. A **warrior** for your city. A **voice** to the nations.

7 FINAL CHARGES FOR THOSE WHO WILL WALK IN DOMINION

1. **Guard your gates**
   Don't reopen spiritual doors through compromise, rebellion,

relationships, or curiosity.
"*Give no place to the devil.*" — Ephesians 4:27

2. **Discipline your appetite**
Fasting should be part of your monthly rhythm. It realigns the soul and keeps your flesh under submission.

3. **Commit to purity**
Emotional, sexual, verbal, visual. Impurity is the number one gate demons use to crawl back in.

4. **Master the Word**
Scripture isn't optional. It's your sword, shield, and daily bread. *"Let the word of Christ dwell in you richly..."* (Col. 3:16)

5. **Find your tribe**
Deliverance was never meant to be walked alone. Build, serve, and heal in a Spirit-filled community.

6. **Embrace suffering**
Yes — suffering. Not all torment is demonic. Some is sanctifying. Walk through it. Glory is ahead.
"After you have suffered a little while... He will strengthen, settle, and establish you." — 1 Peter 5:10

7. **Teach others**
Freely you have received — now freely give. Help others get free. Start with your home, your circle, your church.

FROM DELIVERED TO DISCIPLE

This devotional is a global cry — not just for healing but for an army to rise.

It is **time for shepherds** who can smell warfare.

It is **time for prophets** who don't flinch at serpents.

It is **time for mothers and fathers** who break generational pacts and build altars of truth.

It is **time for nations** to be warned, and for the Church to no longer be silent.

YOU ARE THE DIFFERENCE

Where you go from here matters. What you carry matters. The darkness you were pulled from is the very territory you now have authority over.

Deliverance was your birthright. Dominion is your mantle.
Now walk in it.

FINAL PRAYER

Lord Jesus, thank You for walking with me these 40 days. Thank You for exposing the darkness, breaking the chains, and calling me to a higher place. I refuse to go back. I break every agreement with fear, doubt, and failure. I receive my kingdom assignment with boldness. Use me to set others free. Fill me with the Holy Spirit daily. Let my life become a weapon of light — in my family, in my nation, in the Body of Christ. I will not be silent. I will not be defeated. I will not give up. I walk from darkness to dominion. Forever. In Jesus' name. Amen.

How to Be Born Again and Start a New Life with Christ

Maybe you've walked with Jesus before, or maybe you've just met Him through these 40 days. But right now, something inside you is stirring.

You're ready for more than religion.

You're ready for **relationship**.

You're ready to say, "Jesus, I need You."

Here's the truth:

"For everyone has sinned; we all fall short of God's glorious standard... yet God, in His grace, freely makes us right in His sight."

— Romans 3:23–24 (NLT)

You can't earn salvation.

You can't fix yourself.

But Jesus already paid the full price — and He's waiting to welcome you home.

How to Be Born Again

BEING BORN AGAIN MEANS surrendering your life to Jesus — accepting His forgiveness, believing He died and rose again, and receiving Him as your Lord and Savior.

It's simple. It's powerful. It changes everything.

Pray This Out Loud:

"**LORD JESUS, I BELIEVE You are the Son of God.**
  I believe You died for my sins and rose again.
  I confess that I have sinned and I need Your forgiveness.
  Today, I repent and turn from my old ways.
  I invite You into my life to be my Lord and Savior.

Wash me clean. Fill me with Your Spirit.
I declare I am born again, forgiven, and free.
From this day forward, I will follow You —
and I will live in Your steps.
Thank You for saving me. In Jesus' name, amen."

Next Steps After Salvation

1. **Tell Someone** – Share your decision with a believer you trust.
2. **Find a Bible-Based Church** – Join a community that teaches God's Word and lives it out. Visit God's Eagle ministries online via https://www.otakada.org or https://chat.whatsapp.com/H67spSun32DDTma8TLh0ov
3. **Get Baptized** – Take the next step publicly to declare your faith.
4. **Read the Bible Daily** – Start with the Gospel of John.
5. **Pray Every Day** – Talk to God as a friend and Father.
6. **Stay Connected** – Surround yourself with people who encourage your new walk.
7. **Start a discipleship Process within the community** – Develop one on one relationship with Jesus Christ via these links

40-day discipleship 1 - https://www.otakada.org/get-free-40-days-online-discipleship-course-in-a-journey-with-jesus/

40 Discipleship 2 - https://www.otakada.org/get-free-40-days-dna-of-discipleship-journey-with-jesus-series-2/

My Salvation Moment

Date: _____
 Signature: _____

"*If anyone is in Christ, he is a new creation; the old has passed away, the new has come!*"

— 2 Corinthians 5:17

Certificate of New Life in Christ

Salvation Declaration – Born Again by Grace

This certifies that

_____

(FULL NAME)

has publicly declared **faith in Jesus Christ**
as Lord and Savior and has received the free gift of salvation
through His death and resurrection.

"If you openly declare that Jesus is Lord and believe in your heart that God raised Him from the dead, you will be saved."
— Romans 10:9 (NLT)

On this day, heaven rejoices and a new journey begins.

Date of Decision: _____

Signature: _____

Salvation Declaration

"TODAY, I SURRENDER my life to Jesus Christ.
　I believe He died for my sins and rose again.
　I receive Him as my Lord and Savior.
　I am forgiven, born again, and made new.
　From this moment forward, I will walk in His steps."

Welcome to the Family of God!

YOUR NAME IS WRITTEN in the Lamb's Book of Life.

Your story is just beginning — and it's eternal.

CONNECT WITH GOD'S EAGLE MINISTRIES

- Website: www.otakada.org[1]
- Wealth Beyond Worry Series: www.wealthbeyondworryseries.com[2]
- Email: ambassador@otakada.org

- **Support this work:**

Support kingdom projects, missions, and free global resources through covenant-led giving.

Scan QR Code to Give
https://tithe.ly/give?c=308311

Your generosity helps us reach more souls, translate resources, support missionaries, and build discipleship systems globally. Thank you!

---

1. https://www.otakada.org
2. https://www.wealthbeyondworryseries.com

3. JOIN OUR WHATSAPP Covenant Community

Receive updates, devotional content, and connect with covenant-minded believers worldwide.

Scan to Join

https://chat.whatsapp.com/H67spSun32DDTma8TLh0ov

RECOMMENDED BOOKS & RESOURCES

- ***Delivered from the Power of Darkness*** (**Paperback**) — Buy Here[1] | Ebook on Amazon[2]

- **Top Reviews from the United States:**
  - **Kindle Customer:** "The Best Christian read ever!" (5 stars)

PRAISE JESUS FOR THIS testimony. I have been so blessed and would recommend every one to read this book... For the wages of sin is death but the gift of God is eternal life. Shalom! Shalom!

---

1. https://shop.ingramspark.com/b/084?params=oeYbAkVTC5ao8PfdVdzwko7wi6IQimgJY2779NaqG4e
2. https://www.amazon.com/Delivered-Power-Darkness-AFRICAN-DELIVERED-ebook/dp/B0CC5MM4MV

- **Da Gster**: "This is a very interesting and rather strange book." (5 stars)

If what is said in the book is true then we really are way behind on what the enemy is capable of doing! ... A must for anyone wanting to learn about spiritual warfare.

- **Visa**: "Love this book" (5 stars)

This is an eye opener... a true confession... Recently I have been searching for it everywhere to buy it. So happy to get it from Amazon.

- **FrankJM**: "Quite different" (4 stars)

This book reminds me how real spiritual warfare is. It also brings to mind the reason for putting on the "Full Armor of God."

- **JenJen**: "Everyone who wants to go to Heaven- read this!" (5 stars)

This book changed my life so much. Together with John Ramirez's testimony, it will make you look at your faith differently. I've read it 6 times!

- *Ex-Satanist: The James Exchange* (Paperback) — Buy Here[3] | Ebook on Amazon[4]

---

3. https://shop.ingramspark.com/b/084?params=I2HNGtbqJRbal8OxU3RMTApQsLLxcUCTC8zUdzDy0W1
4. https://www.amazon.com/JAMESES-Exchange-Testimony-High-Ranking-Encounters-ebook/dp/B0DJP14JLH

- **TESTIMONY OF AN African EX-SATANIST** - *Pastor JONAS LUKUNTU MPALA* (Paperback) — Buy Here[5] | Ebook on Amazon[6]

- *Greater Exploits 14* (Paperback) — Buy Here[7] | Ebook on Amazon[8]

---

5. https://shop.ingramspark.com/b/084?params=0Aj9Sze4cYoLM5OqWrD20kgknXQQqO5AZYXcWtoMqWN

6. https://www.amazon.com/TESTIMONY-African-EX-SATANIST-Pastor-Jonas-ebook/dp/B0DJDLFKNR

7. https://shop.ingramspark.com/b/084?params=772LXinQn9nCWcgq572PDsqPjkTJmpgSqrp88b0qzKb

8. https://www.amazon.com/Greater-Exploits-MYSTERIOUS-Strategies-Countermeasures-ebook/dp/B0CGHYPZ8V

- *Out of the Devil's Cauldron* by John Ramirez — Available on Amazon[9]
- *He Came to Set the Captives Free* by Rebecca Brown — Find on Amazon[10]

Other books published by author – Over 500 titles
Loved, Chosen and Whole: A 30-Day Journey from Rejection to **Restoration** translated into 40 languages of the world
https://www.amazon.com/Loved-Chosen-Whole-Rejection-Restoration-ebook/dp/B0F9VSD8WL
https://shop.ingramspark.com/b/
084?params=xga0WR16muFUwCoeMUBHQ6HwYjddLGpugQHb3DVa5hE

---

9. https://www.amazon.com/Out-Devils-Cauldron-John-Ramirez/dp/0985604306
10. https://www.amazon.com/He-Came-Set-Captives-Free/dp/0883683239

In His Steps — A 40-Day WWJD Challenge:
Living Like Jesus in Real-Life Stories Around the World

https://www.amazon.com/His-Steps-Challenge-Real-Life-Stories-ebook/dp/B0FCYTL5MG

https://shop.ingramspark.com/b/084?params=DuNTWS59IbkvSKtGFbCbEFdv3Zg0FaITUEvlK49yLzB

JESUS AT THE DOOR:
40 Heartbreaking Stories and Heaven's Final Warning to TODAY'S Churches

https://www.amazon.com/dp/B0FDX31L9F

https://shop.ingramspark.com/b/084?params=TpdA5j8WPvw83glJ12N1B3nf8LQte2a1lIEy32bHcGg

COVENANT LIFE: 40 Days of Walking in the Blessing of Deuteronomy 28

- https://www.amazon.com/dp/B0FFJCLDB5

Stories from Real People, Real Obedience, and Real https://shop.ingramspark.com/b/084?params=bH3pzfz1zdCOLpbs7tZYJNYgGcYfU32VMz3J3a4e2Qt

Transformation in over 20 languages

KNOWING HER & KNOWING HIM:
40 Days to Healing, Understanding, and Lasting Love

HTTPS://WWW.AMAZON.com/KNOWING-HER-HIM-Healing-Understanding-ebook/dp/B0FGC4V3D9[11]

https://shop.ingramspark.com/b/084?params=yC6KCLoI7Nnum24BVmBtSme9i6k59p3oynaZOY4B9Rd

COMPLETE, NOT COMPETE:
A 40-Day Journey to Purpose, Unity, and Collaboration

---

11. https://www.amazon.com/KNOWING-HER-HIM-Healing-Understanding-ebook/dp/B0FGC4V3D9

HTTPS://SHOP.INGRAMSPARK.com/b/084?params=5E4v1tHgeTqOOuEtfTYUzZDzLyXLee30cqYo0Ov9941[12]
 https://www.amazon.com/COMPLETE-NOT-COMPETE-Journey-Collaboration-ebook/dp/B0FGGL1XSQ/

DIVINE HEALTH CODE - 40 Daily Keys to Activate Healing Through God's Word and Creation Unlock the Healing Power of Plants, Prayer, and Prophetic Action

---

12. https://shop.ingramspark.com/b/084?params=5E4v1tHgeTqOOuEtfTYUzZDzLyXLee30cqYo0Ov9941

https://shop.ingramspark.com/b/084?params=xkZMrYcEHnrJDhe1wuHHYixZDViiArCeJ6PbNMTbTux

https://www.amazon.com/dp/B0FHJT42TK

OTHER BOOKS CAN BE found on author page
https://www.amazon.com/stores/Ambassador-Monday-O.-Ogbe/author/B07MSBPFNX

APPENDIX (1-6): RESOURCES FOR MAINTAINING FREEDOM & DEEPER DELIVERANCE

APPENDIX 1: Prayer to Discern Hidden Witchcraft, Occult Practices, or Strange Altars in the Church

"*Son of man, do you see what they are doing in the dark...?*" — Ezekiel 8:12

"*And have no fellowship with the unfruitful works of darkness, but rather expose them.*" — Ephesians 5:11

Prayer for Discernment & Exposure:

Lord Jesus, open my eyes to see what You see. Let every strange fire, every secret altar, every occultic operation hiding behind pulpits, pews, or practices be exposed. Remove the veils. Reveal idolatry masked as worship, manipulation masked as prophecy, and perversion masked as grace. Purge my local assembly. If I am part of a compromised fellowship, lead me to safety. Raise pure altars. Clean hands. Holy hearts. In Jesus' name. Amen.

APPENDIX 2: Media Renunciation & Cleansing Protocol

"*I will set no wicked thing before mine eyes...*" — Psalm 101:3
Steps to Cleanse Your Media Life:

1. **Audit** everything: movies, music, games, books, platforms.
2. **Ask:** Does this glorify God? Does it open doors to darkness (e.g., horror, lust, witchcraft, violent or new age themes)?
3. **Renounce:**

"I renounce every demonic portal opened through ungodly media. I disconnect my soul from all soul ties to celebrities, creators, characters, and storylines empowered by the enemy."

1. **Delete & Destroy**: Physically and digitally remove content.
2. **Replace** with godly alternatives — worship, teachings, testimonies, wholesome films.

APPENDIX 3: Freemasonry, Kabbalah, Kundalini, Witchcraft, Occult Renunciation Script

"*Have nothing to do with the fruitless deeds of darkness...*" — Ephesians 5:11

Say aloud:

In the name of Jesus Christ, I renounce every oath, ritual, symbol, and initiation into any secret society or occult order — knowingly or unknowingly. I reject all ties to:

- **Freemasonry** – All degrees, symbols, blood oaths, curses, and idolatry.
- **Kabbalah** – Jewish mysticism, Zohar readings, tree of life invocations, or angel magic.
- **Kundalini** – Third eye openings, yoga awakenings, serpent fire, and chakra alignments.
- **Witchcraft & New Age** – Astrology, tarot, crystals, moon rituals, soul travel, reiki, white or black magic.
- **Rosicrucians, Illuminati, Skull & Bones, Jesuit Oaths, Druid Orders, Satanism, Spiritism, Santeria, Voodoo, Wicca, Thelema, Gnosticism, Egyptian Mysteries, Babylonian rites.**

I nullify every covenant made on my behalf. I cut all ties in my bloodline, in my dreams, or through soul ties. I surrender my entire being to the Lord Jesus Christ — spirit, soul, and body. Let every demonic portal be closed permanently by the blood of the Lamb. Let my name be cleansed from every dark register. Amen.

APPENDIX 4: Anointing Oil Activation Guide

"*Is any among you afflicted? Let him pray. Is any sick among you? Let them call for the elders... anointing him with oil in the name of the Lord.*" — James 5:13–14

How to Use Anointing Oil for Deliverance & Dominion:

- **Forehead**: Renewing the mind.
- **Ears**: Discerning the voice of God.
- **Belly**: Cleansing the seat of emotions and spirit.
- **Feet**: Walking into divine destiny.
- **Doors/Windows**: Closing spiritual gates and cleansing homes.

Declaration while anointing:

"I sanctify this space and vessel with the oil of the Holy Spirit. No demon has legal access here. Let the glory of the Lord dwell in this place."

APPENDIX 5: Renunciation of Third Eye & Supernatural Sight from Occult Sources

Say aloud:

"In the name of Jesus Christ, I renounce every opening of my third eye — whether through trauma, yoga, astral travel, psychedelics, or spiritual manipulation. I ask You, Lord, to close all illegal portals and seal them by the blood of Jesus. I release every vision, insight, or supernatural ability that did not come from the Holy Spirit. Let every demonic watcher, astral projector, or entity monitoring me be blinded and bound in Jesus' name. I choose purity over power, intimacy over insight. Amen."

APPENDIX 6: Video Resources with Testimonies for spiritual growth

1) start from 1.5 minutes - https://www.youtube.com/watch?v=CbFRdraValc

2) https://youtu.be/b6WBHAcwN0k?si=ZUPHzhDVnn1PPIEG

3) https://youtu.be/XvcqdbEIO1M?si=GBlXg-c-O-7f09cR

4) https://youtu.be/jSm4r5oEKjE?si=1Z0CPgA33S0Mfvyt

5) https://youtu.be/B2VYQ2-5CQ8?si=9MPNQuA2f2rNtNMH

6) https://youtu.be/MxY2gJzYO-U?si=tr6EMQ6kcKyjkYRs

7) https://youtu.be/ZW0dJAsfJD8?si=Dz0b44I53W_Fz73A

8) https://youtu.be/q6_xMzsj_WA?si=ZTotYKo6Xax9nCWK

9) https://youtu.be/c2ioRBNriG8?si=JDwXwxhe3jZlej1U

10) https://youtu.be/8PqGMMtbAyo?si=UqK_S_hiyJ7rEGz1

11) https://youtu.be/rJXu4RkqvHQ?si=yaRAA_6KIxjm0eOX

12) https://youtu.be/nS_Insp7i_Y?si=ASKLVs6iYdZToLKH

13) https://youtu.be/-EU83j_eXac?si=-jG4StQOw7S0aNaL

14) https://youtu.be/_r4Jyzs2EDk?si=tldAtKOB_3-J_j_C

15) https://youtu.be/KiiUPLaV7xQ?si=I4x7aVmbgbrtXF_S

16) https://youtu.be/68m037cPEu0?si=XpuyyEzGfK1qWYRt

17) https://youtu.be/z4zlp9_aRQg?si=DR3lDYTt632E96a6

18) https://youtube.com/shorts/H_90n-QZU5Q?si=uLPScVXm81DqU6ds

FINAL WARNING: You Can't Play With This

D eliverance isn't entertainment. It's war.
Renunciation without repentance is just noise.
Curiosity is not the same as calling.
There are things you don't recover from casually.
So count the cost. Walk in purity. Guard your gates.
Because demons don't respect noise — only authority.

www.ingramcontent.com/pod-product-compliance
Lightning Source LLC
Chambersburg PA
CBHW030335010526
44119CB00047B/509